Dana DuTerroil | Joni

111 Places
in Houston
That You Must
Not Miss

Photographs by Daniel Jackson

111

To Rosia!
Have fun
exploring
Houston ♡

Ji Dana

emons:

To my family, who have joined me on field trips around the world.
Dana DuTerroil

To Derek and Laurence and the adventures that await us.
Joni Fincham

© Emons Verlag GmbH
All rights reserved
Photographs by Daniel Jackson, except see p. 237
Cover icon: shutterstock.com/M.Aurelius
Edited by Karen E. Seiger
Maps: altancicek.design, www.altancicek.de
Basic cartographical information from Openstreetmap,
OpenStreetMap-Mitwirkende, ODbL
Printing and binding: Grafisches Centrum Cuno, Calbe
Printed in Germany 2021
ISBN 978-3-7408-0896-9
Revised second edition, April 2021

Did you enjoy this guidebook? Would you like to see more?
Join us in uncovering new places around the world on:
www.111places.com

Foreword

Our Houston love stories have two vastly different beginnings. Joni arrived in 2010 as a reluctant new Houstonian, skeptical of finding the city's charms. One particular hot, humid, and mosquito-plagued walk left her wondering why anyone would want to live here. On the other hand, Dana had a head start as a Houston teenager attending the High School for the Performing and Visual Arts during the AstroWorld and Marvin Zindler era. After a long while living in New Orleans, Dana returned in 2008 (just in time for Hurricane Ike). She rekindled old friendships and formed new bonds, including one with a certain Houston transplant.

Sharing her native knowledge with Joni, Dana revealed a city that embraces diversity as a multicultural badge of honor, where an enterprising Vietnamese jeweler supplies the hip-hop scene with bling, while mariachis perform at a church mass. Meanwhile, Houston's blueprint of seeming randomness exposed a Pharaoh's head staring down commuters and former bank buildings that now house an ornate mosque and a storied music club. Therein lies the spirit of Houston.

Our two perspectives as a native and a newcomer are the perfect combination for writing a Houston guidebook for Houstonians. From the inner loop to the outskirts, we sought out the overlooked, unknown, and abandoned. Dana's sentimental journeys provided context for Joni's fresh insights, while we both relished the pursuit of unlikely discoveries, like birding, fly fishing, and polo matches in the midst of the city's infamous urban sprawl. Pushed beyond our respective local experiences, we were exposed to a whole new city. The difficulty wasn't in finding 111 places, but in having to pick so few from so many incredible options.

We hope you enjoy this guide and use it as inspiration for exploring and falling in love with the city, one unique place at a time.

111 Places

1__ 14 Pews

Where cinephiles congregate

The Church of Christ forbids the use of musical instruments, but music resonated in the branch's chapel on Aurora Street in Sunset Heights where the a cappella choir sang every Sunday for 60 years. Following the congregation's departure for a roomier locale, a non-profit microcinema moved in. Twice. First, in 1998, Andrea Grover opened Aurora Picture Show in the former sanctuary where screenings of experimental films were held in lieu of services. Following Aurora's relocation, Houston native and accomplished filmmaker Cressandra Thibodeaux christened the space 14 Pews. She added two inches of stuffing to pew cushions along with 100 pillows for a more comfortable film-going experience.

According to Cressandra, the impeccable acoustics lend the space to song. So along with films, she also turns the intimate stage over to musicians like the creative composers from Nameless Sound for performances and recording sessions. The movie calendar frequently includes music documentaries and festivals devoted to themes like Houston blues history or the theremin, an antenna-like instrument with a sci-fi sound. Other film series celebrate scream queens and female directors, or raise awareness about bullying.

Moviegoers are served drinks by Marilyn, Cressandra's mother, who also doles out chocolate chip cookies in the repurposed collection baskets. The cozy setting encourages post-film discussion and provides an opportunity to view the latest art exhibition hung on the wood-paneled walls.

Although the white wooden church was reborn as a multidisciplinary space, rituals also have their place here. Marriages, including the city's first gay nuptials, and memorials, often in remembrance of local artists, are welcome at 14 Pews. More than a microcinema, this neighborhood theater on a quiet residential street is an inspiring microcosm of tolerance and creativity.

Address 800 Aurora Street, Houston, TX 77009, www.14pews.org, info@14pews.com |
Getting there Bus 44 to North Main & Aurora Street | Hours See website for showtimes |
Tip Enjoy artist-made films, including a festival devoted to young filmmakers from around
the world, at Aurora Picture Show (2442 Bartlett Street, www.aurorapictureshow.org).

2 1910 Courthouse

The original justice league

While most people dread jury duty, you might actually look forward to serving if it's in the Harris County 1910 Courthouse. But there's no need to wait for a summons to visit the only Houston hall of justice listed on the National Register of Historic Places. Even the location has significance. In 1837, the first session of the District Court of the Republic of Texas convened at the site, conducting proceedings outdoors. Four courthouses would occupy the lot of land, which covers an entire city block, and the final one still stands. Despite a 1950s renovation removing much of the decorative magnificence in favor of modernization, an architectural team uncovered the building's original splendor and replicated the rest using historical photographs and records.

Now, over 100 years later, the still functioning, six-story courthouse contains the First and Fourteenth Courts of Appeal, along with visitors serving as grand jurors, and couples tying the knot in the fourth-floor courtroom equipped with balcony seating befitting a Broadway theater. Security officers do double duty as impromptu tour guides, armed with brochures guiding visitors through the palatial surroundings.

The wow factor begins on the main floor with black and white marbled stairs flanking the atrium. A stream of sunlight signals you to gaze upward for the first glimpse of the domed, stained-glass skylight in the rotunda. As you make your ascent, a mix of original and new ironwork and wood requires an eagle eye to spot the difference. Displays detailing the meticulous restoration are on view, plus a photograph of the 1912 legal community, which included two women, who were among the first females licensed to practice law in Texas. For a final blast from the past, inspect the oldest artifact: a cornerstone from the 1884 courthouse, cementing the notion that everything old is new again.

Address 301 Fannin Street, Houston, TX 77002, +1 (713) 274-9683, www.harriscountyarchives.com/Other-Resources/1910-Courthouse-Tours | Getting there METRORail to Central Station Capitol (Green & Purple Line) | Hours Mon–Fri 8am–5pm | Tip Shred for free as long as you're wearing a helmet at the Lee and Joe Jamail skatepark named after its donor, Attorney Joe Jamail, who made litigation history (and $335 million for his services) after securing a $10.53 billion award for Pennzoil in a landmark case held in the 1910 Courthouse (103 Sabine Street, www.houstontx.gov/parks/parksites/leejoepark.html).

3   Abandoned Holy Palace

A suburban white elephant

The Chong Hua Sheng Mu Holy Palace is the misfit of Alief, an unassuming West Houston neighborhood filled with ordinary, midsize apartment complexes and single-story, uniform, brick homes. The five-story, 40,000-square-foot structure dominated by a 40-foot geometric gold orb is a mishmash of Seussian architecture and Mesoamerican pyramids. Its arresting contrast against the surrounding prefab landscape makes it impossible to catch a glimpse of the palace and not wonder why it exists.

The Wu-Wei Tien Tao Association, a local Chinese Universalist sect, built the palace for a $6-million-dollar price tag in 1999 as part of an envisioned 11-acre compound containing housing, retail, and a day-care center. Weeks away from completion, construction on the project suddenly halted when a series of complicated events left the religious group in disarray. After their elderly founder died suddenly, the new leader, Kwai Fun Wong, accompanied the body to Hong Kong for burial according to custom. However, Wong was in the process of applying for US citizenship and failed to obtain permission to leave the country. Upon her return, she was arrested and eventually deported. Subsequent lawsuits, internal drama, and power struggles ensued.

While the building's fate remains uncertain, someone is watching over it, painting over the occasional graffiti, mowing the lawn, and maintaining the parking lot. After 18 years, if there are any remaining loyal Tien Taoists, it's unlikely they will complete their dream temple. Hopefully, the striking shrine can avoid demolition (the common destiny of so many vacant buildings in Houston) and continue to spark the imagination of the casual observer. And just maybe a creative real estate mogul will snatch up this crazy construction and realize its true purpose as a new age observatory and spa for astrologists and tarot readers.

Address 3695 Overture Drive, Houston, TX 77082 | Getting there Bus 25 to Ashford
Point & Ashburnham Drive | Hours Unrestricted from the outside | Tip Iglesia La Luz
Del Mundo is the largest church in the US of the Mexico-based Pentecostal denomination
bearing the same name, meaning "Light of the World." The massive, Pantheon-like structure
topped with a large gold dome has been intriguing commuters along Interstate 59 since
2005 (8312 Eastex Freeway).

4 Ad Astra

Actually, it IS rocket science

Propelling humankind to the next generation of space travel is the goal of a small company based three miles from NASA in an unassuming building behind a strip mall housing a hibachi grill, reflexology studio, and an H&R Block. Ad Astra Rocket Company is the brainchild of Franklin Chang Díaz, a plasma physicist and retired astronaut. As the first Latin American NASA astronaut, he shares the record for most spaceflights with seven shuttle missions over his impressive 25-year career. Now, he and his team of rocket scientists are developing the Variable Specific Impulse Magnetoplasma Rocket (VASIMR®) engine, a technology that will exponentially increase our ability to travel farther, faster, and cheaper in space.

Facility tours are led by a member of their super-smart staff, who are skilled at taking big scientific concepts and breaking them down into understandable nuggets, even peppering in pop culture references, like how their research saved Matt Damon in *The Martian*. The laboratory is dominated by the gigantic vacuum chamber, where the magic of turning neutral gases, like argon or xenon, into plasma fuel that burns as hot as the Sun's surface takes place. If the engine is firing, visitors can climb a stepladder to peek inside the viewing window that reveals the plasma's mesmerizing light show.

The applications for the VASIMR® engine are as exciting as the technology itself. Ad Astra's rockets can serve as space garbage trucks, collecting orbital debris. As the semi-trucks of space, the rockets will haul supplies and cargo to space stations and future moon colonies. They can even protect Earth from total demise by nudging an incoming asteroid off its collision path. And as we become a multi-planet species, their technology will eventually help us reach new space cities in warp drive time.

So be sure to stop by their gift shop because you'll want a souvenir of this future history.

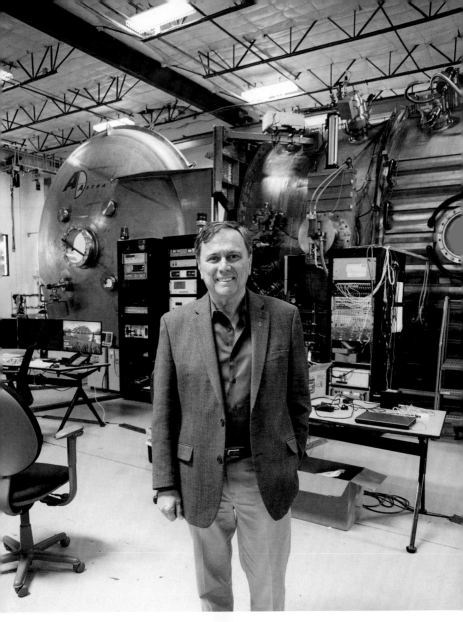

Address 141 West Bay Area Boulevard, Webster, TX 77598, +1 (281) 526-0500,
www.adastrarocket.com, info@adastrarocket.com | Getting there By car, Southbound
Interstate 45 to exit 26, left onto Bay Area Boulevard, right at Samurai Japanese Steak,
continue behind the strip mall | Hours Tours by appointment only | Tip View the
heavens from the James Turrell skyspaces on Rice Campus (moody.rice.edu/james-turrell-
twilight-epiphany-skyspace) and the Live Oak Meeting House (1318 West 26th Street,
www.houstonquakerskyspace.com).

5 — The Alley Theatre
All the drama that goes on backstage

Find out what goes on in the dirty props room during a behind-the-scenes tour of the Tony Award-winning Alley Theatre, the second-oldest resident company theater in the United States. You'll also learn of the theater's humble beginnings in a small dance studio with a sycamore tree rooted in the middle – they provided umbrellas for the audience on rainy performance nights. A long, narrow alleyway leading to the studio inspired the theater's name.

The tour twists and turns through the maze of offices, workshops, dressing rooms, rehearsal studios, and stages in the theater's current home, a Brutalist sandcastle building designed specifically for The Alley in 1968. The twice-flooded theater underwent major renovations to protect their top-of-the-line production facility. A two-toned blue wall in the basement marks the devastating water levels with one yellow line for Tropical Storm Allison in 2001 and another for Hurricane Harvey in 2017, just below the ceiling.

Safely relocated high atop the parking garage, the "theater-making laboratory in the sky" allows visitors to see the beehive of activity that creates each production. Walk past carpenters busy building elaborate sets in the enormous scene shop with 56-foot ceilings, actors waiting for fittings in the costume shop, and shelves filled with taxidermy, swords, antiques, and other props awaiting stage duty.

In the lobby, guides point out otherwise unnoticed architectural details, like the interlocking "A"s that create the triangle skylight, and the Texas oak banisters. Backstage of the Alley's main theater reveals the inner workings of the fully trapped stage floor and computerized fly loft. You may catch a glimpse of the Lady in White, the theater's ghost in a vintage dress, whose brief appearances always take place at stage left. Her origin story is unknown, but she often reveals herself to visiting actors. Perhaps she'll grace your tour group with her presence.

Address 615 Texas Avenue, Houston, TX 77002, +1 (713) 220-5700, www.alleytheatre.org | Getting there Bus 85, 160, 161, 162, 218 to Smith Street & Texas Avenue | Hours Daily noon–6pm, tours by appointment | Tip During the annual Theater District Open House, seven of Houston's top cultural and performing arts spaces open their doors to the public for tours, special performances, and activities, all for free (www.theaterdistrictopenhouse.com).

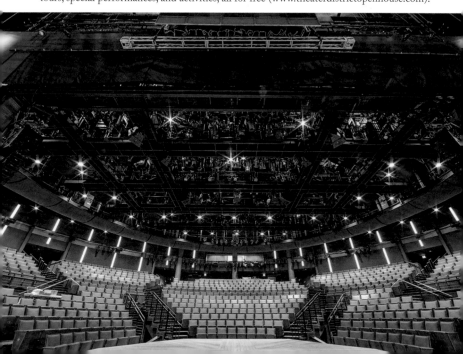

6 Art Car Museum

Honk if your car is covered in crustaceans

Considering how much time Houstonians spend in traffic, it's no wonder the Art Car movement of the 1980s caught on in a city with commute times averaging 59 minutes round trip. As an art form, art cars are a magical metamorphosis, creating an aesthetic sensibility from an inanimate, practical object. These moveable works of art come in all forms – a 1967 Ford Country sedan festooned with plastic fruit or a Toyota RAV transformed into a bright red hippo with a wagging tail. Houston is the Art Car Capital of the World, and it's a welcome sight to spot a mobile masterpiece on the road as you navigate the city's 669 square miles.

You can also view these creative cars up close at the Art Car Museum, aka the Garage Mahal. Start at the head-turning scrap metal and chrome exterior designed by David Best, an artist known for his temporary, elaborate temples at Burning Man. Since the museum's opening in 1998, a variety of art cars have been on display here, including the Roachster, a 30-foot-long, drivable cockroach made of steel with antennae that burn fire, and Rex the Rabbit, a demonic Easter Bunny perched on top of a Volkswagen Rabbit, of course. Many of these works of art on wheels participate in the yearly Art Car Parade each spring, when over 250 creations cruise the streets. Beyond featuring art cars, the museum is dedicated to showcasing outsider and non-traditional contemporary artists with a yearly open call. The resulting show features the first 100 registrant artists and has no entry fee.

Whether you're a spectator or a creator, the community spirit embodied in the art car world adds a layer of soul to our concrete jungle. This spirit is also present in the gallery named in memory of T. Mitchell Jones, the former curator who was fatally struck by a drunk driver outside of the museum in the early morning hours after the 2008 Art Car Parade.

Address 140 Heights Boulevard, Houston, TX 77007, +1 (713) 861-5526,
www.artcarmuseum.com | Getting there Bus 40 to Heights Boulevard & Center Street |
Hours Wed–Sun 11am–6pm | Tip View provocative and politically charged art with
an emphasis on local and regional artists at the Station Museum of Contemporary Art
(1502 Alabama Street, www.stationmuseum.com).

7 Asia Society Texas

Blending in through the rising mist

When Asia Society Texas Center opened in 2012, Museum District neighbors called 911. Believing the fog rising from the second-floor terrace was smoke signaling a five-alarm fire, residents later learned the visual effect was an element of the building's design. But it's not uncommon for Yoshio Taniguchi, the center's architect, to draw attention, whether it's a museum in his native Japan or his 2004 renovation of MoMA in New York City. However, over-the-top ornamentation or avant-garde construction is not Taniguchi's method of operation. Transcendence is more his style.

For the center, an educational and cultural institution fostering connection between Houston and the Asia-Pacific region, Taniguchi relied on the concept of "borrowed scenery," where natural materials like water, stone, and wood camouflage urban distractions, like delivery trucks. In doing so, his first freestanding building in the United States works with the environment, not against it.

Taniguchi's architectural illusion is best viewed from the Water Garden Terrace windows on the second floor. Through the eight-foot glass panes so crystal clear that discreet stickers were placed on them to prevent collisions, see mist rising every 13 minutes, briefly forming clouds blocking out city life. Texas heritage oak trees on the front lawn form a forest, with the downtown skyline symbolizing a mountain range, albeit manmade. Even the parking lot hides an underground geothermal system, minimizing unsightly air-conditioning ductwork.

By creating a clean slate with walls of Jura limestone, meticulously selected by Taniguchi, who rejected 90 percent of the dinosaur-age slabs, the center's art exhibitions, lectures, and performances remain the focal point. But, when you see visiting Tibetan monks craft an annual mandala from grains of colorful sand with painstaking precision, think of Taniguchi.

Address 1370 Southmore Boulevard, Houston, TX 77004, +1 (713) 496-9901, www.asiasociety.org/texas | **Getting there** METRORail to Museum District (Red Line) | **Hours** Tue–Fri 11am–6pm, Sat & Sun 10am–6pm | **Tip** Natural materials are also the foundation of Hermann Park's Japanese Garden, designed by the late landscape architect Takeshi "Ken" Nakajima (6001 Fannin Street, www.hermannpark.org/poi/24).

8 The Beer Can House

An uncanny landmark

Creative upcycling aptly describes the Beer Can House. This modest, three-bedroom bungalow covered in over 50,000 flattened aluminum cans is the work of John Milkovisch, a beer-loving Houstonian who tired of his property's upkeep. In 1968, John built a covered patio to provide a shady spot to pop a cold one with his friends and wife Mary. He added a fence created from a stockpile of 28,000 multicolored marbles to sparkle in the sun as decor. Although later destroyed in a hurricane, the fence served as the genesis for this revered American roadside attraction.

The Beer Can House's transformation continued with weekend projects until John's retirement in 1976 allowed him to devote his days to building his idiosyncratic monument. He didn't like mowing the grass, so he covered the yard in cement decorated with inlaid marbles and stones. The pull tabs of the couple's collection of empty beer cans were strung into garlands and hung along the roof's eaves to shade the house from the Texas sun, with the added bonus of creating a meditative jingling sound in the breeze. Never wanting to paint the house again, John flattened the cans and fashioned sheets of siding to cover the exterior.

Mary went along with her husband's eccentric hobby, helping him drink beer and contributing plastic fruit trees for the yard which only survive in photos. But she forbade any cans on the home's interior claiming it as her domain. John's artistry inside the house consists of hand-cut linoleum floors, tiled backsplash, and an intricate inlaid-wood counter where the guest book currently resides.

After John's death in 1988, Mary remained in the house, welcoming curious passersby. The family ensured that John's aluminum magnum opus would live on by entrusting it to the guardians of Houston's quirky art scene, The Orange Show Center for Visionary Art (see ch. 71).

Address 222 Malone Street, Houston, TX 77007, +1 (713) 926-6368, www.orangeshow.org/beer-can-house | Getting there Bus 20 to Memorial Drive & Asbury Street | Hours See website for seasonal hours | Tip Start your own beer can collection with a visit to D & Q The Beer Station's sizable selection of craft beers from Texas and around the world. Peruse the humorous tasting notes for their small but unique wine section and enjoy the neon fish aquariums while you wait to pay (806 Richmond Avenue, twitter.com/TheBeerStation).

9 __ Blood and Money Mansion
Death by chocolate éclair

Palatial residences and coiffed lawns dominate Houston's fancy River Oaks neighborhood. But murder is also part of the moneyed scenery. Set in a Southern Colonial mansion, a true crime cast features an oil tycoon patriarch, his beautiful socialite daughter, and her philandering, plastic surgeon husband accused of killing her with poisoned pastries. Hitchcock blonde Grace Kelly would have been a dead ringer to play Joan Robinson Hill, the fetching equestrian who succumbed to a sudden, suspicious illness at the age of 38. Instead, *Murder in Texas*, the 1981 TV movie based on the bestselling book *Blood and Money* starred Texas-born Farrah Fawcett, as the leading lady. Sam Elliott played Dr. Hill, who was awaiting a retrial when he was murdered during a robbery at the home in what many considered a hit ordered by Ash Robinson, Joan's vengeful father, portrayed by Andy Griffith.

While the actual home of this upper crust whodunnit didn't make it to the big screen like *Amityville Horror*, the white-bricked estate maintains its murder mystery curb appeal. Even from a distance, the windows of Dr. Hill's lavish music room are visible, but you'll have to imagine the hand-painted fresco on the ceiling. From the street, you can look past the imposing iron gate and baroque fountain to see the front door where the doctor was gunned down.

Known as an area with real estate listings to die for, this phrase hit close to home for the wife of a high-end bookie who was shot 13 times in her five-bedroom abode. Other scenes of high society scandal include the River Oaks Country Club, where cradle-robbing octogenarian Howard Marshall II canoodled with his young bride-to-be Anna-Nicole Smith. Members of the Enron gang also hid out in this affluent enclave, like deceased kingpin Kenneth Lay, who lived in a penthouse with nine bathrooms, six elevators, and ten parking spaces.

Address 1561 Kirby, Houston, TX 77019 | Getting there Bus 41 to Kirby & Pine Valley Drive | Hours Unrestricted from outside only | Tip Joan Robinson Hill was a fierce competitor at the Pin Oak Charity Horse Show, considered one of the most prestigious horse shows in the Southwest. The event is held every spring as a fundraiser for Texas Children's Hospital (2501 South Mason Road, Katy, www.pinoak.org).

10 _Books of a Feather_

Let your imagination soar

Perched outside the Alice McKean Young Neighborhood Library, three sparkling, enormous birds welcome visitors to the light-filled community space. The mosaic masterpieces are the work of local artist, Dixie Friend Gay, who draws inspiration from nature and the tradition of animals as icons in ancient mosaics. Unlike her other murals beautifying public parks and buildings throughout the city, *Books of a Feather* comes to life in 3-D form – each bird measures 10 feet long, 6 feet wide, and 12 to 15 feet in height depending on its decorative head plumage.

The vibrant ceramic and glass tiles creating the multi-shaped feathers were all laid by hand in sheets at Friend's home studio in The Heights, while construction of the steel frame and bodies took place at the studio of David Adickes, whose specialty is larger-than-life sculptures (see ch. 66). Stamped into the birds' colorful wings is a reading list referencing birds, wings, and flight. The book titles, ranging from *The Ugly Duckling* fairy tale to the Western classic *Lonesome Dove*, were gathered from the local community and library personnel's suggestions, as well as a few of the artist's own favorite literary works.

With the birds' inquisitive facial expressions inspiring flights of fancy, *Books of a Feather* is the finishing touch to the state-of-the-art building constructed in 2016, a short distance from the library's original 1957 location on Griggs Road. The library's namesake, Alice McKean Young, was one of Texas' earliest suffragettes, who also used her political savvy to advocate for more city libraries. Dedicated in her role as dean of the Houston Public Library Board, Young held her final meeting from her deathbed. No doubt she would appreciate the bright and airy design of the new building that embraces the increasingly important role that neighborhood libraries play in their communities.

Address 5107 Griggs Road, Houston, TX 77021, +1 (832) 393-2140, www.houstonlibrary.org/location/young-neighborhood-library | Getting there METRORail to Palm Center Transit Center (Purple Line) | Hours Sculpture unrestricted; see website for library hours | Tip Welcoming visitors to Midtown Park is Friend's *Wild Wonderland*, a 64-foot-long mosaic mural depicting Houston's flora and fauna in impressive detail (corner of Anita Street and Main Street).

11   Boulevard Bird Watching

High-flying society

The most exotic residents in the posh Boulevard Oaks neighborhood don't live in the stately mansions along the red-bricked esplanades, but rather high up in the neighborhood's signature live oaks. The yellow-crowned and black-crowned night herons arrive in mid-February and make themselves at home through June, when they begin their migration back to the tropics of Central and South America. Considering the number of bayous in the vicinity, it's a peculiar choice for a heronry, but the night herons have been nesting here for decades.

A flurry of activity kicks off the breeding season. The males make a spectacle of themselves courting a mate. Then the pairs work together to build their nest among the tangled branches of the nearly century-old trees. Watching the strikingly elegant parents in their graceful behaviors for weeks, it's shocking to see the straggly, dinosaur-like baby chicks peeking from the nest. As the chicks grow bigger, they get feisty with their siblings, fighting over space and food, while some even resort to fratricide, tossing the others out of the nest. Before learning to fly, the awkward juvenile herons can be seen using their wings and feet to climb up the trees and learning to hunt tadpoles in curbside puddles.

Local birders flock to the neighborhood to observe these amazing creatures – some get set up for the duration with lawn chairs, binoculars, and cameras. Not everyone welcomes the night herons though. Their cacophony of loud squawks disrupts the normally tranquil boulevards. The ground is littered with rotting aquatic debris and lizard carcasses from their messy eating. Pedestrians must beware of the large white patterns of splatter on the sidewalks indicating a nest above. However, with the snowy and great egret populations settling in the area, perhaps the herons can blame the mess on the new birds on the block.

Address North, South, & West Boulevards in Boulevard Oaks, Houston, TX 77006 |
Getting there Bus 65 to Bissonnet & Mandell Street | **Hours** Unrestricted | **Tip** A surprising
hotspot for urban birding is the small Russ Pitman Park due to the turn-of-the-century
pecan grove and other plantings that remain from a former family estate. Be on the lookout
for hummingbirds, warblers, thrushes, tanagers, and even parrots (7112 Newcastle Street,
Bellaire, www.naturediscoverycenter.org/russ-pitman-park).

12 Brennan's of Houston

Oscar-winning date night

Book a table for two at Brennan's and re-enact the boozy lunch where Jack Nicholson told Shirley MacLaine she would need a lot of drinks to kill the bug up her ass in the Academy Award winning film, *Terms of Endearment*. The cinematic tearjerker, based on the book by native Texan Larry McMurtry, was filmed in Houston with the swanky River Oaks neighborhood as the backdrop. But one of the most memorable scenes went down at Brennan's, which is why the *Terms of Endearment* table is still requested by regulars. The intimate dining space – just nine tables – is also a fan favorite with views of the restaurant's French Quarter courtyard.

The New Orleans ambience is no accident. Brennan's of Houston opened in 1967 as the sister restaurant to Commander's Palace, the Creole fine dining landmark in New Orleans. The family tree even extends to the restaurant's physical location, originally designed in the 1920s by noted Houston architect John Staub for the Junior League. Staub took inspiration from a French Quarter residence that would, in an act of architectural coincidence, become Brennan's of New Orleans in 1956. With gas lanterns and decorative wrought iron out front, plus pralines as a post-meal *lagniappe* by the door, the Creolization of Houston was complete.

Southern hospitality overflows with 25-cent martinis at lunch, yellow sashes on tables signaling a celebration, and Brennan's signature Bananas Foster flambéed tableside. Many of Houston's top chefs got their start making 35-gallon batches of snapping turtle soup here, including James Beard Award-winning chef Chris Shepherd. On any given day, you might witness a wedding proposal in front of the courtyard fountain, Saints fans taking in a game at the bar, friends feasting at the chef's table in the kitchen, or a jazz trio at Sunday brunch, all reminding patrons what it means to miss New Orleans.

Address 3300 Smith Street, Houston, TX 77006, +1 (713) 522-9711, www.brennanshouston.com | Getting there Bus 82 to Elgin & Smith Street | Hours See website for hours | Tip Stroll the grounds of Rienzi, home to the Museum of Fine Arts' European decorative arts collection in a former residence, also designed by John Staub (1406 Kirby Drive, www.mfah.org/visit/rienzi).

13 Buffalo Soldier Headdress

Warriors of the western frontier

The intricately beaded suit with a feathered headdress on display at the Buffalo Soldier National Museum was never worn in battle. Instead, the garment, hand sewn by a Mardi Gras Indian from New Orleans, honors the military might of this unsung branch of the United States Armed Forces. Michael Dow Edwards, "Spyboy Dow" of the Mohawk Hunters, created the suit depicting scenes of the brave African-American soldiers named by the Plains Indians for their valor during the American-Indian Wars. Each piece of the suit tells a story of the special relationship forged between Native Americans and the Buffalo Soldiers, including the feathers bearing the distinct blue and yellow of the Buffalo Soldier uniform.

In the same way, the museum, housed in a former armory, brings the story of the Buffalo Soldiers to life. They first served as protectors of settlers and cattle herds during the westward expansion. In 1866, Congress established six African-American military regiments consisting of cavalry and infantry units. The nickname would subsequently refer to all African-American soldiers through World War II. A nickname even bestowed on one woman who defied the prohibition against females serving in the military at that time by concealing her identity and enlisting in the 39th Infantry. Through artifacts and artwork, the world's largest collection of African-American military memorabilia enlightens visitors beyond the lyrics of the popular Bob Marley song.

The exhibitions also highlight the achievements of modern-day Buffalo Soldiers, including astronauts. In 2006, the Buffalo Soldier flag was flown aboard the *Discovery* with Mission Specialist Stephanie D. Wilson on board. A poignant display in memory of the flying Buffalo Soldiers Michael P. Anderson and Ronald McNair, killed on the Columbia and Challenger space missions, reminds us all of their tremendous valor.

Address 3816 Caroline Street, Houston, TX 77004, +1 (713) 942-8920, www.buffalosoldiermuseum.com, info@buffalosoldiermuseum.com | Getting there Bus 291 to San Jacinto & Holman Street | Hours Mon–Fri 10am–5pm, Thu 1–5pm (free admission), Sat 10am–4pm | Tip View artwork and attend cultural events informed by the African-American experience at the Houston Museum of African American Culture (4807 Caroline Street, www.hmaac.org).

14 The Cactus King

Beware the cactus' kiss

No open-toed shoes or flip-flops allowed at the world's largest public retailer of cacti and succulents. Situated on five acres with 15 greenhouses, The Cactus King functions like a working farm in the middle of the city. All their plants are grown on location from seeds or propagations, often from mother plants that are decades old. The inventory of roughly 2,000 species of cacti and succulents, which includes rare, variegated varieties and 80-year-old *Astrophytums*, attracts botany students and horticulturists from around the world, along with locals looking for a new house plant or two.

The small staff is extensively trained in the necessary skills to care for these precious plants, like watering schedules, soil conditions, and the proper way to carry a heavy and pointy, yet delicate cactus without dropping it.

The Cactus King's clientele are mainly online orders, walk-in customers, and landscape architects, but zoos, botanical gardens, special collectors, and movie production companies also seek out their expertise. Landscape services are available, but there's a two-year waitlist. Pricing varies by rarity, size, and time and resources required to cultivate the plant. Baby ones cost as little as a few dollars, while "unicorns" will go for $8,000 or more.

The Cactus King is an extension of the owner Lyn Rathburn's personality: frugal, resourceful, and artistic. He lives on-site in an off-the-grid shipping container at the back of the property. The nursery repurposes everything, from bottle caps used to secure the ground tarps blocking out weeds to old garden hoses sculpted into a *Looney Tunes* cactus. When Rathburn takes a break from living his botany dream, he creates works of art from his personal salvage yard amassed over the years. His junkyard installations spotted throughout the nursery are just as unique and worthy of a visit as the Cactus King's collection of botanical treasures.

Address 7900 I-45 North, Houston, TX 77037, +1 (281) 591-8833, www.thecactusking.com | Getting there By car, Interstate 45 Northbound to exit 57A Gulf Bank Road | Hours Mon–Sat 9am–6pm | Tip For something less prickly, the floral shops on Fannin Street's Flower Row (between Wentworth and Wichita Streets) offer deals on rose bouquets, seasonal arrangements, and memorial displays.

15 ___ Cactus Music

BYOG (Bring Your Own Glass)

With pint glasses in hand, regulars head inside local music club-house Cactus Music for their frequent and free in-store events featuring meet-and-greets and short sets by local and touring bands on a humble stage. Fans watch the bands from the aisles surrounded by bins filled with compact discs, record albums, and even cassettes. This unsung venue in the city is really the best place to see an intimate show by your favorite musicians or discover a group before they start headlining summer festivals. Catering to a wide variety of tastes, the store's busy calendar showcases genres from country and western to punk.

Creative fan events are one of the reasons Cactus Music has been in business for 45 years, outliving many of their industry counterparts and the alt weeklies that bestowed it with annual awards for Best Music/Record Store. The in-store events hail from the Saturday on-air radio performances hosted at Daily's Record Ranch, the illustrious music store started by country music pioneer Pappy Daily in 1946. Appearances included then-undiscovered artists like Hank Williams, Texas Troubadour, Ernest Tubb, and Hank Thompson, the King of Western Swing.

When Pappy's sons opened Cactus Music in 1975, they continued the tradition of in-store events with the likes of The Ramones, The Police, Patti Smith, Townes Van Zandt, Alice Cooper, Phillip Glass, Jeff Buckley, Steve Earle, and Sleater-Kinney all taking part over the years. As a tribute, the vinyl department is named the Record Ranch, where large photos of these remarkable performances hang on the wall just behind the DJ station.

Music-themed art shows, author signings, and listening parties are just a few of the other ways Cactus Music creates a gathering space for the city's music lovers. As for the pint glasses, those are for the two free St. Arnold's beers poured for adult customers at every event.

Address 2110 Portsmouth Street, Houston, TX 77098, +1 (713) 526-9272, www.cactusmusictx.com | **Getting there** Bus 27 to South Shepherd Drive & Richmond Avenue | **Hours** Mon–Sat 10am–9pm, Sun noon–7pm | **Tip** For more free beer, visit Vinal Edge (239 West 19th Street, www.vinaledge.com), which hosts in-store concerts and participates in a monthly sip and stroll, or Deep End Records' Punk Rock Garage Sales, Cheap Date Art Shows, and VHS Swap Shops (708 Telephone Road, Suite C, www.facebook.com/DeepEndHTX).

16__CAMH's Open Studio
Come in and express yourself

On the first Saturday of the month, visitors entering Contemporary Arts Museum Houston (CAMH) become the artists. Since 2008, CAMH's open studio sessions invite visitors of all ages to exercise their creative muscles with hands-on activities inspired by current exhibitions. If you've ever stared at a work of art and said, "My kid could do that," well now your child can give it a try. Visitors often end up making this monthly creative endeavor a family affair. And take note: open studio is a critique-free zone.

Past projects include building a power medallion, assembling box kites, and still-life sketching of delightfully deranged dolls. Because the themes riff on the exhibitions, open studio events are planned six months in advance. The artists themselves occasionally make an appearance too. Such innovative programming creates continuity and community at a museum that does not have a permanent collection.

While CAMH's corrugated stainless steel parallelogram building looks built to last, the art on display is not meant to stay. Even Mel Chin's *Manilla Palm*, a 60-foot artificial tree with fiberglass fronds planted on the west lawn, is on a long-term loan. Unlike CAMH's Museum District neighbors, CAMH acts as a *kunsthalle* – a non-collecting institution embracing the European tradition of exhibition rather than accumulation. Some of CAMH's past exhibits have utilized materials with a short shelf life, like loaves of bread, ice, and plants, so these works would not have fared well in a permanent collection.

Despite the seemingly fleeting nature of CAMH's approach, the museum has a solid reputation for exhibiting emerging artists whose names are now instantly recognizable, such as painter Julian Schnabel and photographer Cindy Sherman. Perhaps the amateur artists attending an open studio will leave a lasting impression on CAMH's walls too.

Address 5216 Montrose Boulevard, Houston, TX 77006, +1 (713) 284-8250, www.camh.org, info@camh.org | Getting there METRORail to Museum District (Red Line) | Hours Tue, Wed & Fri 10am–7pm, Thu 10am–9pm, Sat 10am–6pm, Sun noon–6pm; open studios first Saturday of the month 2–4pm | Tip Resident artists at the Houston Center for Contemporary Craft have an open-door policy where you can see the creative process at work (4848 Main Street, www.crafthouston.org).

17 Camp Logan Rebellion
When push comes to shove

The city's largest greenspace, Memorial Park, is named in honor of the armed forces who fought in Europe during World War I. On land where marathon runners and bicyclists now roam once stood Camp Logan, a training base for troops, established in 1917. However, the Black members of the 3rd Battalion, 24th Infantry who guarded Camp Logan during its construction never saw any action overseas. While the military afforded Black men the opportunities for advancement denied to them on the civilian side, the soldiers sent to Houston, after just battling Pancho Villa, faced a home-grown enemy.

The soldiers, whether on duty at Camp Logan or stationed at their nearby segregated camp, encountered a daily campaign of racial harassment inflicted by city cops and bigoted locals. Forbidden to carry their sidearms in public, the soldiers sought refuge in the welcoming Fourth Ward, home to the Black nightlife scene. But the men were reminded of their second-class status as they endured verbal abuse on the streetcar ride back to base camp.

On August 23, 1917, a rumor spread among the soldiers that a corporal had been murdered by Houston police officers when he intervened in the beating and arrest of a fellow soldier. United by anger, an armed rebellion of 100 soldiers formed. As the soldiers marched to police headquarters downtown, they clashed with police and civilians; 16 people were killed and 22 injured, less than a month after the soldiers set foot in the city. After the largest murder trial and court martial in history, 19 soldiers were sentenced to hang, and 53 were imprisoned for life.

Camp Logan closed in 1919, and the headlines of the violent mutiny were left in the past – until 1992, when a historical marker was placed at the training ground's original entrance, noting the role Camp Logan played in fighting injustices abroad and at home.

Address Find marker in Memorial Park at the corner of Arnot and Haskell Streets, Houston, TX 77007 | **Getting there** By car, from the Washington Avenue roundabout, take the second exit onto Arnot Street and then turn right on Haskell Street | **Hours** Daily 6am–11pm | **Tip** The soldiers never reached downtown, but they marched past College Memorial Park Cemetery, founded in 1896, which serves as the resting place for Black leaders, including two soldiers killed during the rebellion – the Buffalo Soldiers National Museum placed markers on their graves (3525 West Dallas, www.collegeparkcemetery.org).

18 __ Casa Ramirez

Mi casa es tu casa

Help yourself to some *polvorones*, cookies dusted with cinnamon sugar, because for Chrissie and Macario Ramirez, their folk art gallery is a second home. On a block teeming with Main Street nostalgia, Casa Ramirez brings Latino culture. Inspired by his father's craftsmanship, Macario set up the shop to showcase arts and crafts in the Heights, his longtime neighborhood, where he died peacefully at home in 2020 at the age of 86. Local and regional artwork shares space with woven bags bearing the likeness of Frida Kahlo and *lotería* cards updated for the millennial set. As the number of dual language schools has increased in the area, the couple added more bilingual books to their inventory.

The store has a strong seasonal draw when customers come in for heart-shaped *milagros* on Valentine's Day and traditional tin ornaments from Oaxaca at Christmas. But don't go looking for Halloween décor because the skeletons and skulls on display represent *Día de los Muertos*, or Day of the Dead, the most important holiday on the Casa Ramirez calendar. This widespread celebration in Mexico, featuring a blend of pre-colonial indigenous customs and Catholicism, is held on November 1st and 2nd to honor deceased loved ones.

Macario's respect for *Día de los Muertos* also came from his father, who taught him the traditions. Macario paid the lesson forward with free classes in October to prepare the community for the ritual that, in his words, "belongs to all of us." Students learn to make a personal *ofrenda* (altar), and they study the symbolism within the celebration. Inside the shop, people contribute personal offerings to a community altar. The lessons culminate in a procession, where participants carry photos of their dearly departed against the backdrop of marigold crosses. Teaching these traditions seems to be working, as Chrissie notices more kids, upon seeing the colorful skulls, responding, "Coco!" rather than "Boo!"

Address 241 West 19th Street, Houston, TX 77008, +1 (713) 880-2420, www.casaramirez.com, casa.ramirez@att.net | Getting there Bus 26 to West 20th & Rutland Street | Hours Tue–Fri 10am–5pm, Sat 10am–6pm, Sun noon–5pm | Tip Pick up Mexican pastries at El Bolillo, where Casa Ramirez stocks up on *pan de muerto* during *Día de los Muertos* (multiple locations, www.elbolillo.com).

19__Celestis Memorial Spaceflights

Fly me to the moon, but not back

If you don't have the right stuff for NASA's Astronaut Candidate Program, there's still an opportunity to suit up. But there's a catch. Your space flight will take place in the afterlife.

Over the last 20 years, Celestis Memorial Spaceflights has conducted 16 missions carrying the cremated remains and DNA samples of space geeks, sci-fi fans, New Agers, and their dogs into the cosmos. Most famously, the Celestis Founder's Flight in 1997 beamed up *Star Trek* creator Gene Roddenberry and 60s LSD counterculture luminary Timothy Leary, along with 22 other passengers on a Pegasus rocket.

Charlie Chafer, Celestis co-founder and interstellar travel agent, mans this innovative space program from an office that is open by appointment only. Inside, screens display live tracking of Celestis flights currently in orbit, which can be seen online. Clients from 30 different countries have booked flights, including a local TV reporter who covered NASA. Framed commemorative patches from past missions hang on the wall, along with a *New Yorker* cartoon depicting a family of mourners at a rocket launch with the caption, "Bye-bye, Grandma."

In reality, only one to seven grams of the dearly departed take flight, enclosed in a specially designed, personally engraved flight capsule, referred to as the "secondary payload" on spaceflights. The capsules piggyback on rockets and satellites with flight packages ranging from a round trip or a permanent celestial journey into deep space starting at $12,500. However, the honorary crew's remains leave no trace as their capsules are either recovered and returned to loved ones or absorbed by the atmosphere upon the spacecraft's reentry. Like a shooting star, this is a stellar send-off only Space City could bestow.

Address 3801 Kirby Drive, Suite 540, Houston, TX 77098, +1 (281) 971-4019, www.celestis.com, cs1@celestis.com | Getting there Bus 25 to Richmond Avenue & Kirby Drive | Hours By appointment only | Tip Hunt for a copy of Lew Merrill's 1941 paperback *Space Burial* at Third Planet, the second-oldest sci-fi comic and collectible store in the US (2718 Southwest Freeway, www.third-planet.com).

20 Chapel of St. Basil

A teachable moment

At noon, three bronze bells toll from atop the Chapel of St. Basil at the University of St. Thomas, announcing the Angelus, a daily call to prayer for Catholics. It's a moment of serenity, when the ringing of bells reorients student life from the scholarly to the spiritual. The intellectual and ecclesiastical come together on campus, and the most striking example is on the University Mall.

Designed by architect Philip Johnson in 1956, the Mall's green space is surrounded by brick buildings facing each other as a united academic front, anchored by the library on one end of the quadrangle. Over 40 years later, Johnson came out of retirement at the age of 84 and returned to the Mall to design a sacred space, a far cry from the skyscrapers defining his style and Houston's downtown skyline.

The Chapel's location, directly across from the library, completes the union of academia and faith in a work of architecture that begins as a geometry lesson. A stark white stucco cube forms the body of the Chapel, a sphere of 24-karat gold-leaf serves as the dome, and an intersecting black granite plane joins the two elements.

The Chapel's façade, facing the Mall rather than the busy street, also emphasizes the campus connection while alluding to the Old Testament with a tent flap design signaling a place of sanctuary. Inside, St. Basil, the Chapel's namesake, is portrayed as a teacher, painted by a Polish iconographer. Mary's shrine, titled *The Seat of Wisdom*, shows her on a throne, sculpted in bronze, with the child Jesus on her lap holding the Gospels.

Students come to the daily mass, and, in fact, it was their blue jeans that led to the addition of cushioned pews to prevent the rivets on their pockets from scratching the black walnut surface. The Chapel also sees an uptick in attendance during exams – further proof of the higher education and higher power connection.

Address 1018 West Alabama Street, Houston, TX 77006, +1 (713) 525-3589, www.stthom.edu/About/Chapel-of-St-Basil.aqf, campusministry@stthom.edu | Getting there Bus 56, 298 to Montrose Boulevard & West Alabama Street | Hours Unrestricted from the outside; see website for mass schedule | Tip Philip Johnson, along with architects Howard Barnstone and Eugene Aubry, designed the nearby Rothko Chapel, an interfaith sanctuary and meditation destination containing 14 paintings by Mark Rothko (3900 Yupon Street, www.rothkochapel.org).

21 _ Colorado Plaza Sign

The neon lights are big and bright

Scenic activists have long lamented the visual blight cluttering Houston's cityscape. With approximately 4,000 lanes of interstates and expressways, there's a lot of ad space available. Billboards compete for attention from motorists, whose eyes are easily diverted by oversized American flags waving from car dealership parking lots. Churches use enormous symbols of faith for curb appeal, like the 170-foot-tall cross gracing the Beltway.

However, there's one standout among the onslaught of signage. At dusk, drivers along the Southwest Freeway are treated to visual stimulation seemingly imported from the Las Vegas Strip. At first blush, the neon-lit Colorado Plaza sign, accompanied by jewel-toned kinetic whorls, conjures up visions of casinos and buffets of prime rib. Children, mesmerized by the light show, beg their parents to pull over for what is surely a Chuck E. Cheese on steroids.

While the 52-foot-high sign leaves a lot to the imagination, the business behind the ambiguous name decidedly does not. In 1993, the Colorado Sports Bar and Grill, a self-proclaimed strip pub, contracted Industrial Neon Sign, a local company that's been designing and restoring neon signs since 1934, to create the sign that area businesses now use as a directional landmark.

Set against a mirrored finish, undulating rose and purple neon lights frame the 4-foot-tall letters in a frenzy of prismatic, scintillating action. The sign, which took approximately two months to construct, would cost about a million dollars today, not including the hefty power bill.

Inside the Colorado's wild game themed interior, a wall of fame includes alums-turned-centerfolds, including the late Anna Nicole Smith. Dancers perform on baby grand pianos, receiving tips from patrons who've made use of the dollar bill dispensing ATM. A glimpse of the neon lights outside is a much cheaper thrill.

22 DeBakey Library & Museum

Mender of broken hearts

Most people hope to avoid a visit to the Texas Medical Center, Houston's medical metropolis easily identified by the large number of scrubs and white coats sported by the doctors, nurses, and support staff who work along the complex's two-mile stretch near downtown. As the world's largest medical district, the number of patient visits range in the millions, with over 180,0000 surgeries performed each year.

By far the most celebrated of those surgeries were those carried out by the late, trailblazing heart surgeon, Dr. Michael E. DeBakey, whose accomplishments all seem to start with firsts – from inventing the roller pump to keep weak hearts beating to the coronary artery bypass. You can follow the timeline of his cardiovascular contributions in his namesake museum which opened in 2006 on the campus of the Baylor College of Medicine, where DeBakey became the school's first and longest-serving chair of the Department of Surgery.

An interactive surgical suite shows off where DeBakey demonstrated his surgical prowess, but a nearby photo reveals what might have been the most important tool in the doctor's life: his wife's sewing machine. Applying the sewing skills his mother taught him, DeBakey crafted artificial arteries by hand from Dacron, otherwise known as polyester, which served as the model for his pioneering aortic graft.

The most famous heart surgeon in the world also had many VIPs as patients. Autographed photos from thankful US presidents, royals, and Vegas headliners with blocked arteries are on display, including Marlene Dietrich showing off her famously well-insured legs, which DeBakey repaired. But the most important signatures are found in the guestbook that sits on DeBakey's desk as you enter the museum. In it, you'll find the names of past and future medical students, ensuring that DeBakey's legacy of medical innovation keeps on ticking.

Address 6450 East Cullen Street, Houston, TX 77030, www.bcm.edu/about-us/our-campus/debakey-museum | Getting there METRORail to Memorial Hermann Hospital/Houston Zoo (Red Line) | Hours Mon–Fri 9am–5pm | Tip While the 64-foot-tall Williams Tower Water Wall (2800 Post Oak Boulevard) is showered with attention, the Texas Medical Center also features a towering wall of cascading water lining the exterior of the J. P. McGovern Texas Medical Center Commons (6550 Bertner Avenue).

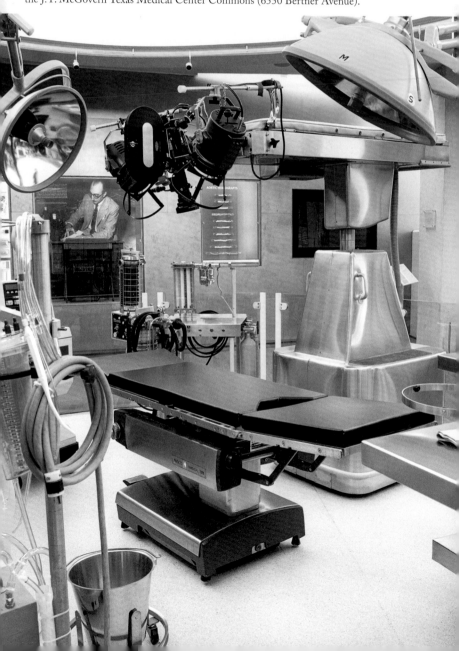

23 Doug's Barber Shop

Lights, camera, action, and cut!

The most famous movie set in Houston is a barber shop that's been in continuous operation since 1929. Native Houstonian and indie-film director Wes Anderson set several scenes for his breakout movie, *Rushmore*, in the barber shop, which he outfitted with retro Christmas décor. While other Houston locations featured area high schools, like Wes' alma mater, St. John's, standing in for Rushmore Academy, Doug's is the most accessible to movie buffs. Since the film's release in 1998, fans from as far away as Japan have made the trek to see where Bill Murray got a shave and a haircut. While most *Rushmore*-inspired visits involve taking a picture and picking up a business card as a cinematic souvenir, there's plenty more to see in this barber shop.

The current owner and barber Jeff Armstrong purchased the shop in 2014 from Doug, who still came in to cut hair before he passed in late 2020. Jeff also retained Doug's funky folk art aesthetic, covering the walls and ceiling with finds scored on heavy trash days and at church garage sales. Alongside *Rushmore* memorabilia and barber-themed comic strips, Doug's commissioned portrait of the shop's interior by local artist Anna Reese-Hernandez captures the charming time capsule inside. Historic newspaper headlines announcing hurricanes and JFK's assassination give customers something to read as well.

As for haircuts, they're cash only, walk-in only, with a discount for seniors. Jeff sizes up newcomers like a seasoned maître d', pairing hipster beards with the right barber for the job. Royal family bobbleheads adorn one barber's station, and another barber's signature move includes relaxing tense shoulders with a vintage Stim-U-Lax massager. Razor shaves are on the menu, plus buzz cuts and fanciful fades. Many regulars who received their first haircut at Doug's return with their young sons, creating a family tradition for generations.

Address 219 East 11th Street, Houston, TX 77008, +1 (713) 862-0670, www.dougsbarbershop.com | **Getting there** Bus 40 to Heights Boulevard & East 11th Street | **Hours** Mon 8am–6pm, Tue–Fri 8am–7pm, Sat 8am–5pm, Sun 9am–5pm | **Tip** Susan Venus, owner of Venus Hair, keeps a Cadillac hearse sporting a paint job of colorful cats out front and styles mile-high hair designs inside for those wanting a costumed coif (361 West 19th Street, www.venushairhouston.com).

24__The Dr. Jack Express

Take a trippy kiddie train ride

Toot! Toot! All aboard the Dr. Jack Express for an 18-minute journey around the highlights of historic Hermann Park's 445 acres. Upon leaving Kinder Station, the main train depot, the perky audio provides small tidbits of history and information as you go chugging along the two-mile track. Rumble past Jim Love's anatomically correct *Portable Trojan Bear* sculpture, catch a glimpse of the 30-foot mount in the picturesque McGovern Centennial Gardens, and scout out a lawn spot for an evening at Miller Outdoor Theatre, Houston's open-air performance space with a calendar of events ranging from Bollywood productions to zydeco music. If you're lucky, a *quinceañera* photo shoot will be taking place as you pass between the 740-foot reflection pool and the Sam Houston Monument standing tall since 1925.

Halfway through, the ride turns psychedelic in the tunnel where the walls are the unlikely setting for *Destination Mound Town*, a weird and wondrous dreamscape by renowned local artist Trenton Doyle Hancock. Passengers travel through a day in the life of Mounds, mythical half-human, half-plant creatures that populate much of Hancock's art. Originally part of Art in the Park, Hermann Park's 100th birthday celebration in 2014, the tunnel is technically a temporary installation without an end date.

Hermann Park railroad has been delighting guests of all ages since 1954 when its inaugural "train," a tractor pulling two carts, took visitors around the zoo at a whopping two miles per hour. Upgraded and expanded over the years, the popular park amenity now uses two scale replicas of the famous 1863 C. P. Huntington steam locomotive for its engines. The "Engineer for the Day" experience allows train superfans of any age to help with safety checks on these models before riding along all day and performing the challenging task of ringing the bell and blowing the train whistle.

Address 6102 Hermann Park Drive, Houston, TX 77030, +1 (713) 524-5876, www.hermannpark.org/visit/train-pedal-boats, info@hermannpark.org | **Getting there** METRORail to Hermann Park/Rice U (Red Line) | **Hours** See website for seasonal hours | **Tip** Embedded along the Hermann Park Lake Plaza walkway near Kinder Station are small bronze faces, crystal candleholders, and other urban archeological pieces of Houston, put there by local African-American sculptor Jesse Lott, known for his repurposing of found objects.

25 — The Eagle's Phoenix Room

A tribute to Houston's LGBTQ+ history

From the Eagle's original 1970 roost in New York City, the Levi's and leather gay bar spread its wings with branded outposts around the world. While Houston Eagle was late in joining the party, officially opening in 2014, it's the only Eagle with a Phoenix Room.

An electrical fire during happy hour nearly destroyed the bar in 2016. During the rebuild, the idea for an upstairs bar dedicated to sharing the defining moments in Houston's LGBTQ+ history took flight. The intent was an intimate space for quiet conversation. Instead, the Phoenix Room is where the party starts and ends Friday through Sunday.

Above the bartenders mixing stiff cocktails is a timeline of both tragic and celebratory LGBTQ+ milestones, from the brutal local murder of Paul Broussard that brought national attention to anti-gay hate crimes, to the "Love Wins" marriage equality Supreme Court decision. Elder clubbers regale companions with stories of their favorite past hangouts, while perusing the collage of old posters from the Montrose neighborhood's bygone LGBTQ+ institutions, although it's unlikely any of them frequented the Wagon Wheel, a female impersonator club in the late 1930s.

This informal museum's most treasured piece is the recreated iconic mural that once adorned the side of Mary's, the unofficial capital of Montrose. A sentimental place for many patrons, it was a sanctuary during the AIDS epidemic – a place for both activism and mourning. After the bar closed in 2009, the sassy scene depicting bar regulars was painted over. But now you'll find Mary's fans reminiscing in front of the Phoenix Room's replica, redone by the original artist, Scott Swoveland.

Get down on the main dance floor – the testing grounds for the Billboard-topping remix duo, Dirty Disco. And pop in the gift shop selling whips, thruster rings, Pringles, and souvenir T-shirts.

The Gay Press (1968-2016)
HoustonLGBTHistory.org

Address 611 Hyde Park Boulevard, Houston, TX 77006, www.eaglehouston.com | **Getting there** Bus 82 to Westheimer & Stanford Street | **Hours** Mon–Fri 4pm–2am, Sat & Sun noon–2am; Phoenix Room Fri & Sat 9pm–2am, Sun 4pm–2am | **Tip** In front of Blacksmith, the coffeeshop now occupying the building that was Mary's, is a mini mural homage to Swoveland's mural.

26 Eclectic Menagerie Park

Heavy metal pipe dreams

Yes, atop a giant crane is a gorilla waving in your rearview mirror. Barreling southbound on an industrial stretch of Highway 288, you wouldn't expect to see an art haven of massive metal sculptures on the property of the largest pipe-distributor in the US. Family-owned and operated since 1918, Texas Pipe & Supply is the perfect convergence of industry, art, and Houston's freewheeling and generous spirit.

The company's Eclectic Menagerie Park began in 2000, when art lover and third generation chairman Jerry Rubenstein rescued a one-ton hippo from an El Campo concrete plant and placed it in the open field next to the pipe yard along the feeder road. Soon a rhino followed; next, Snoopy piloting a biplane arrived to oversee the site. Now, the ever-expanding collection of over two dozen sculptures, both commissioned and adopted, creates a habitat for oversized stray and bizarre pipe pets. Many of the works are creations by Ron Lee, the beloved, unofficial artist and welder-in-residence, who died in 2017. His *Game of Thrones*-esque dragon, stealth bomber, Mr. Pete the Roadrunner, and well-endowed Alligator Man all exhibit his incredible talent of turning scrap metal into masterpieces.

Impressive as this head-turning roadside attraction is while cruising down the highway, for a truly in-the-field experience, book a tour with Fay Adam, longtime employee and Rubenstein's personal assistant. As the open-air museum's enthusiastic docent, she describes the origin of each work of art. For example, the dinosaur is a tribute to Rubenstein's mother Evelyn who loved to read books to the kids when she wasn't running the company, while the rustic iron mariachi band was rescued from a shuttered Mexican restaurant. Every sculpture tells a story, often with a connection to Houston and its residents, providing us all with inspiration to get on the road again.

Address 2330 Holmes Road, Houston, TX 77051, +1 (800) 233-8736, www.texaspipe.com/about/eclectic-menagerie-park | Getting there By car, State Highway 288 Southbound to exit Bellfort Avenue | Hours Visible from highway, call to schedule a tour | Tip When the historic Teas Nursery closed in 2009, the Rubenstein brothers, Jerry and Maury, purchased the land to create a park in honor of their mother. Evelyn's Park Conservancy features a butterfly garden, art lawn, and a whimsical, interactive *Alice in Wonderland*-themed sculpture (4400 Bellaire Boulevard, Bellaire, www.evelynspark.org).

27 The Eldorado Ballroom

Stomping down on Dowling Street

Before being renamed Emancipation Avenue in 2017, Dowling Street was the main drag of the Third Ward. During its heyday, the street was alive with Black-owned businesses and a happening nightlife scene. You can envision the sharply-dressed crowds headed to their favorite juke joint for a soul-soothing evening of music and dancing. Still standing on the corner of Elgin and Dowling Streets, just across from Emancipation Park, is the historic Eldorado Ballroom, the crown jewel of Houston's blues and jazz scene during its reign.

From 1939 until the club's closure in the early 1970s, the "'Rado," its local nickname, was the cornerstone of the Black community. Talent shows and sock hops drew crowds weekly along with a big name roster of blues, jazz, and R&B performances by the likes of B.B. King, Count Basie, Etta James, Ray Charles, and Ike and Tina Turner. Local real estate investor and savvy businesswoman Anna Dupree and her husband Clarence opened the club as a classy venue for affluent Black people, whose entertainment options in the city were limited at that time by Jim Crow laws.

The 'Rado was also where local legends launched their careers, like Johnny "Guitar" Watson and Sam "Lightnin'" Hopkins, whose own historical marker is right at the corner of Francis Street and Emancipation Avenue. A raconteur both on and off stage, Hopkins was known for his irregular guitar rhythms and spontaneous lyrics that often referenced his audience or simply the weather outside. Living in the area, he was a fixture on Dowling Street and often found drinking in bars by day and playing on stage at night. But as much as this prolific bluesman, whose discography includes over 100 recordings and some 600 songs, loved the stage, he was just as happy playing porch concerts for anyone who would listen. The Eldorado Ballroom became a part of Project Row Houses (see ch. 78) in 1999.

Address 2310 Elgin Street, Houston, TX 77004, https://projectrowhouses.org/space-rental | **Getting there** Bus 09 to Elgin & Hutchins Street | **Hours** See website for occasional events | **Tip** Visit Paradise Cemetery South (16001 Cullen Boulevard), where two Houston blues legends and former bandleaders at the Eldorado Ballroom are buried: tenor saxophonist Arnett Cobb (block 1, plot 26s, space 2) and Conrad "Prof" Johnson (block 1, plot 284n, space 6), who wrote *Howling on Dowling*.

28 __ Enron's big E

No longer the smartest guy in the room

Houston strip malls are often overlooked as run-of-the-mill real estate. However, these unremarkable shopping centers frequently give credence to the phrase, "Don't judge a book by its cover." Across the city, tenants range from James Beard-nominated chefs to worshippers of the Hindu god Ganesh. And in a strip mall off the Gulf Freeway, the physical manifestation of greed sits behind the front desk in a chiropractor's office next door to an adult video outlet and a law firm.

Enron. The Houston-based energy mafia lorded over Wall Street in the 1990s and marked their territory with a giant "E" set at an angle. It was designed by Paul Rand, the man behind the famous logos for IBM and UPS. The Houston Astros played at a ballpark branded Enron Field. However, when news footage of FBI agents collecting evidence from Enron's downtown headquarters was followed by massive local layoffs and an enormous bankruptcy, Enron's name became mud.

Most of Houston has been scrubbed clean of Enron signage. The company's skybridge-connected complex is simply referred to by a street address. Minute Maid took over the naming rights for the baseball stadium. But one stainless steel, five-foot-tall vowel symbolizing the swindling syndicate still remains, albeit behind closed doors.

In 2002, an auction unloading all things Enron culminated in a bidding war for the infamous "E." The owner of Microcache, a computer repair shop, bested a local condo developer with a final bid of $44,000. Now, customers dropping off laptops at the shop for a new hard drive have the unexpected perk of seeing the "E," lit up in red, green, and blue and bolted to a stand that bears the shop's name in a clever rebranding twist. Upon request, curious onlookers may peek at the "E," now on display in the neighboring chiropractor's office – where no amount of adjustments will ever make that crooked signage straight.

Address 6302 Gulf Freeway, Houston, TX 77023, +1 (713) 645-2455 | Getting there By car, I-45 South, exit 41B | Hours Mon–Sat 9am–6pm by request | Tip General Norman Schwarzkopf is a familiar face to patients of Dr. Tinh V. Tran, who served with Stormin' Norman during the Gulf War. A statue depicting the then-colonel's heroics in Vietnam stands in the parking lot as the doctor's tribute to his fellow soldier (2420 Dunlavy Street).

29 __ Ensemble Theatre

Where the "E" stands for everyone

For over 40 years, the African-American experience has taken center stage at the Ensemble Theatre, making it the oldest owned and operated African-American theater in the Southwest. Tired of playing cliché roles, like a butler, George Hawkins set out to create more diverse opportunities for Black actors and artists in the Houston theater scene by starting his own touring company in 1976, The Black Ensemble Company. Initially operating out of the trunk of his Cadillac, Hawkins found the company its first permanent home in a tiny, brick, Midtown building that required scenery to be designed to include a hidden green room for the actors to change between scenes. Now with its own space, the company was renamed The Ensemble Theatre.

In 1985, to accommodate a growing audience and expanding mission, The Ensemble Theatre moved to a former car dealership a few blocks away on Main Street, where it remains today. On performance nights, the large showroom windows are filled with patrons who support the theater's dynamic roster of productions that include world premieres; reimagined classics like *A Christmas Carol*, where Scrooge is a Harlem slumlord; and modern musicals, aka *raparettas*, that feature beatboxing, hip-hop dance, and a live DJ.

The Ensemble Theatre's prestigious acting alumni boasts names like Solange Knowles and *Grey's Anatomy*'s Chandra Wilson, who is also known to take in a performance when she is in town. The Young Performers Program, a series of performing arts camps, fosters the talents of the next generation of actors to grace the theater's stage. Keeping to the company's touring roots, the theater still brings its work to the people, reaching more than 30,000 children and seniors each year with performances, like *Uncle Remus' Br'er Rabbit* and *I, Barbara Jordan*, that share the universal human experience through the stories of African Americans.

Address 3535 Main Street, Houston, TX 77002, +1 (713) 520-0055, www.ensemblehouston.com | Getting there METRORail to Ensemble/HCC (Red Line) | Hours See website for performance and box office schedule; tours by appointment | Tip See the cutting-edge, pay-what-you-can performances from Catastrophic Theatre, along with other community ensembles, who share the stages at the collaborative mixed-arts space, MATCH (3400 Main Street, www.matchouston.org, www.catastrophictheatre.com).

30 Exotic Pop
The thirst-quenching taste of nostalgia

Inside an ordinary Busy Bee gas station on Old Spanish Trail is an extraordinary kiosk of sodas and snacks. Bygone brands and rare flavors of beverages from around the world fill the refrigerated cases next to shelves of hard-to-find cereals, exotic chips, tiramisu Oreos, and limited edition Skittles All White. Colorful portraits of Houston rappers, celebrities, and Imdad, the affable gas station owner, surround the display at Busy Bee, the most popular location in the city for Exotic Pop and its sister company Exotic Snacks.

A friend asked founder Charleston Wilson to bring him some sodas not available in Texas while commuting from Houston to Louisiana for work. After seeing his friend sell them for a profit at his barbershop, Wilson's entrepreneurial instincts kicked in, and he started Exotic Pop out of the trunk of his car. At first, some people balked at the $3 price tag. But would they drive to Lake Charles for a Barq's French Vanilla, Fanta Peach, or Sprite Tropical fix? Moving to vending machines, Exotic Pop's first setup inside Watkins Grocery Store was decorated with images of Houston's legendary DJ Screw (see ch. 88), who famously rapped about "dirty Sprite," linking the brand to the hip-hop scene.

With endorsements from the likes of local rapper Paul Wall and Canadian sensation and Houston-phile Drake (who was won over with a Clearly Canadian care package), Wilson turned his side hustle into a lifestyle brand, with global customers and celebrities clamoring for limited supplies of unique sodas and snacks that serve as status symbols more than treats.

While most soda connoisseurs can't afford their personal vending machines with hologram art and a touch screen for custom orders like superfan Travis Scott, they can visit Busy Bee to indulge in a $30 bottle of Canada Dry Peach Ginger Ale or sample Wilson's personal favorite, Snapple Banana.

Address Busy Bee Mobile Gas Station, 3354 Old Spanish Trail, Houston, TX 77021, +1 (832) 538-0636, www.exoticpop.com | **Getting there** Bus 28 to Old Spanish Trail & Del Rio Street | **Hours** Open 24 hours | **Tip** For more novelty sweets and sodas, visit Rocket Fizz, where you can buy soda flavors like sweet corn, ranch dressing, or Martian poop (7620 Katy Freeway, Suite 315, www.rocketfizz.com/locations/rocket-fizz-houston-tx).

31 Fantasy Coffins of Ghana

Don't fear the reaper

Cremation and embalming equipment. Vintage hearses with show-room shine and gleaming grills. Memorial programs of the rich and famous, including both papal and presidential send-offs. These are all likely subjects for display in the National Museum of Funeral History, established by Robert L. Waltrip, founder and chairman emeritus of Service Corporation International, the largest provider of funeral and cemetery services in the US. The museum opened in 1992 to educate the public about all things funerary.

What visitors might not expect to see while wandering the museum's 30,500 square feet of exhibit space is the largest collection of fantasy coffins outside of Ghana, the West African country where the custom originated. The museum purchased 12 hand-carved coffins from a private collection to showcase the unique burial practice in which the deceased transitions to the great beyond in a dream mobile reflecting the individual's personality, occupation, or aspirations. For the Ga people who practice this custom, death is seen as a continuation rather than completion of a journey.

Meant for burial six feet under, the fantasy coffins put a different spin on the museum's motto: "Any day above ground is a good one." A wooden, painted bull awaits a cattle rancher, while a fish eagle, weighing 220 pounds and measuring eight feet by four feet, would carry a hunter to the heavens. Credited with developing the fantasy design concept, Ghanaian sculptor Kane Quaye, who died in 1992, also crafted symbols of wealth and leisure with a Mercedes-Benz and KLM jetliner providing first-class service to the dearly departed.

Functional yet fun, these vibrantly colored vessels stand in stark contrast to the basic black associated with Western funeral traditions. And if you feared touring a funeral museum would be a downer, the fantasy coffins will leave you high on the afterlife.

Address 415 Barren Springs Drive, Houston, TX 77090, +1 (281) 876-3063, www.nmfh.org, contact@nmfh.org | Getting there By car, I-45 North to exit 64, continue on the feeder road to Barren Springs Drive | Hours Mon–Fri 10am–4pm, Sat 10am–5pm, Sun noon–5pm | Tip Inspired to start a career in embalming or funeral directing? The Commonwealth Institute of Funeral Service next door to the museum hosts open houses twice a year for prospective students (415 Barren Springs Drive, www.commonwealth.edu).

32　The First Mission Control

From Russia with love

At the edge of Gragg Park, a modest green space filled with musical playground equipment, colorful elephant statues, walking trails, and ball fields, sits a building that screams mid-century modern with green stonework and architectural horizontal lines. A quick peek inside the refurbished structure from 1956 reveals a time capsule with glass walls looking out to the lush interior courtyard and wood-paneled hallways with mint green linoleum floors. While most Houstonians know the historic Farnsworth & Chambers Building as the Houston Parks and Recreation Department headquarters, space geeks know it as the first home of NASA.

Having already proved space flight possible with two successful manned flights as part of the Mercury Program at Langley Air Force Base in Virginia, the NASA astronauts, scientists, and engineers moved into their new Houston control center in 1962 with the mission to put a man on the moon. All that science needed more room than was available in the building, so NASA leased various office buildings around Houston until moving into its current home, Johnson Space Center in Clear Lake, just south of the city, in 1964.

Even though park rangers and horticulturists now occupy the offices and conference rooms, the building's important contribution to the city's rich space history is not forgotten. Sitting on the lawn adjacent to the entrance are two spaceman buddies. A bronze statue of Russian cosmonaut Yuri A. Gagarin joyfully outstretching his arms to the sky stands next to a two-dimensional, metal-pointillism mural of American astronaut John H. Glenn, Jr. in his *Friendship 7* Mercury spacecraft. Two Russian-based cultural foundations gifted the artworks to Houston in 2012 as a memento of the famous space race between the USA and Russia and as a tribute to both countries' continued contributions to space exploration.

Address 2999 South Wayside, Houston, TX 77023, +1 (832) 395-7000, www.houstontx.gov/parks/parksites/graggpark.html | **Getting there** Bus 40 to Telephone Road & Wheeler Street | **Hours** Unrestricted from the outside | **Tip** "Houston, Tranquillity base here. The Eagle has landed," Neil Armstrong's immortal first words spoken on the Moon greet visitors in 15 different languages at Tranquillity Park, where space-themed features commemorate the successful Apollo 11 mission (400 Rusk Street, www.downtownhouston.org/guidedetail/parks/tranquility-park).

33 Founder's Memorial

Trouble will find him

Poor William Wallace Rice. He was the victim of not one, but two illicit wills, one more deadly than the other. Chloroformed by his valet in a conspiracy conceived by a wily New York lawyer trying to steal his money, Rice's ashes are now entombed in the granite base of the memorial statue erected in his honor on the main quadrangle at Rice University, the institution his fortune ultimately founded – but not without a fight.

A shrewd merchant and businessman, Rice quickly capitalized on all the commercial opportunities a young Houston had to offer – cotton, railroads, real estate, you name it – making him one of the richest men in the state, and a target. It was his second wife, Elizabeth Baldwin, and her family who first tried to usurp Rice's $200,000 promise to start his namesake institute, claiming common property to his assets upon her death. Protesting Baldwin's will, Rice eventually won, but not without encountering lawyer Albert T. Patrick, who would go on to forge a will awarding *himself* the lion's share of Rice's estate and pursue the aforementioned fatal poisoning. However, the plot was uncovered, and Rice's murder was the subject of many headlines in 1900. After years of litigation, Rice's bequest was finally honored, and Rice University opened in 1912.

Today, you can visit the scenic campus' Academic Quad and pay your respects to the stoic statue affectionately known as Willy, who is now the focal point for homecomings and graduations. The students have adopted him as an unofficial mascot and adorn him with seasonal hats and costumes.

But he's still a mark for mischief. In 1988, a crew of 11 clever students pulled off an incredibly complex prank, lifting the one ton figure off its base and turning it 180 degrees during the dark of night til the early morning. As the sun rose the next day, Rice viewed his school's library for the first time.

Address 6100 Main Street, Houston, TX 77005, +1 (713) 348-0000, www.rice.edu, welcome@rice.edu | Getting there Bus 56, 291, 292, 298 to Main Street & Sunset Boulevard | Hours Unrestricted | Tip The land for Elizabeth Baldwin's namesake park in Midtown was purchased and donated to the city using funds from her estate's negotiated settlement in 1905. Look for the 1912 fountain named after her aunt, Charlotte Baldwin Allen, aka the matriarch of Houston (1701 Elgin Street, www.houstontx.gov/parks/parksites/baldwinpark.html).

34 Freedmen's Town Labyrinth

Walk on sacred ground

At first glance, the ancient practice of labyrinth-making seems an unlikely project for Houston's Fourth Ward neighborhood, known as Freedmen's Town. As Houston's version of Harlem, this African-American enclave had its heyday and peaked in the 1920s. Segregation followed by gentrification pitted the area against preservationists who still struggle to save vestiges of this historic African-American community. However, a sector of serenity exists in the form of the Freedmen's Town Labyrinth, built on the remains of Mount Carmel Missionary Baptist Church and founded by formerly enslaved residents. Condemned for demolition because of the building's structural instability, the church was reborn in 2014 to welcome those seeking inner peace.

Led by labyrinth designer and artist Reginald Adams and labyrinth coach Jay Stailey, a team of students, plus 150 volunteers, constructed a labyrinth on the church's former prayer garden using bricks from the church. The medieval labyrinth in France's Chartres Cathedral served as the spiritual blueprint for the 11-circuit labyrinth – indicating the number of times the path goes around the center. Four mosaic-tiled benches offer an opportunity for rest and contemplation in each of the labyrinth's bastions. At sunset, the colors of the sky cast a mirrored reflection on downtown's skyscrapers, creating a spectacular view rooted in the past.

In Greek mythology, a labyrinth imprisoned the beastly Minotaur in what was more of a maze than a place of meditation. Here, however, the labyrinth is meant to free the mind with no rules to follow, with a 4th-century reminder from Saint Augustine, *Solvitur ambulando*, or "It is solved by walking." A sign also advises visitors that the labyrinth's entrance and exit is one and the same with a path always leading to the center, each step as unique as the individual walking it.

Address 1407 Valentine Street, Houston, TX 77019 | **Getting there** Bus 32 to Gray & Valentine Street | **Hours** Unrestricted | **Tip** The tranquil grounds of Villa de Matel, the Sisters of Charity of the Incarnate Word's Convent, contain a Labyrinth Prayer Walk open to all daily 9am–8pm (6510 Lawndale Street, www.sistersofcharity.org/ruah-spirituality-center/labyrinth).

35 Gallery Auctions

The best little auction house in Texas

Auctioneer Vikki Vines' gift for witty banter and the thrill of a bargain entice customers from all over the country to experience Gallery Auctions' Monday sales, one of Houston's last weekly auctions. Eager buyers arrive early to survey the antiques, furniture, décor, art, and bric-a-brac all piled high in the cavernous warehouse before the action begins. Sitting on her stand with gavel in hand, Vines orchestrates the fast-paced chaos of calling out bids, while her team of handlers hoist, flip, and tilt the items up for sale – Vanna White meets circus strongmen. Paddles pop up and down as attendees vie for their coveted piece.

From a young age, Vines learned to see value in everything, a skill she acquired from her father. She once stopped her mom from tossing a broken crayon so her father could fix it. He used his Zippo to melt the ends and put it back together. That fix-it-up mentality, along with her natural inclination for sales, helped Vines go from a flea market stand to an auction house importing shipping containers packed with goods handpicked on her travels to Europe and South America.

Assisted by her son Jon, whose specialty is mid-century modern furniture, Vines continues to expand Gallery Auctions' inventory and events. Frequent Saturday sales focus on unique lots, like hundreds of designer handbags or once-in-a-lifetime estate sales, including those of famous heart surgeon, Dr. Denton Cooley, and Lonnie Frankel, antique magic prop collector and owner of now-closed Frankel's Costume. Themed soundtracks and pop-up bars add to the atmosphere for these special sales.

Having always welcomed the public, Gallery Auctions is the perfect place to dip your toes into the auction world. Curious shoppers don't even have to register for a paddle; you can simply take in the sights and sounds. However, it's unlikely you'll go home empty-handed.

Address 13310 Luthe Road, Houston, TX 77039, +1 (281) 931-0100, www.galleryauctions.com, email@galleryauctions.com (V.Vines #6153) | Getting there By car, Hardy Toll Road North to exit Aldine Mail Route Road/Aldine Bender Road | Hours Previews Wed–Fri 9am–4pm, auctions Mon 9am; see website for special auctions | Tip Shop for one-off home furnishings at Reeves Antiques, a 14,000-square-foot showroom in Montrose. The family-owned and operated dealer specializes in mid-century modern furniture and fine art from Texas artists (2415 Taft Street, www.reevesantiqueshouston.com).

36__ Glenwood Cemetery Heroes

Houston's Bravest, fallen in the line of duty

One of the most sought-after gated communities in the city consists of an 88-acre leafy expanse where the inhabitants dwell six feet underground. Established in 1871, Glenwood Cemetery overlooks the banks of Buffalo Bayou with landscaped grounds canopied by live oaks providing shade to visitors who once picnicked among the tombstones – a Victorian era pastime from when cemeteries were the functional equivalent of public parks. The cemetery markers bear the names of Houston elites from back in the day, referred to as "the notable interred" on the Glenwood membership rolls. Their namesakes are big buildings: Hobby, Brown, Wortham. The grave of aviation magnate and famous germaphobe Howard Hughes is the star attraction.

Less famous but more poignant is a small parcel dedicated to those who put their lives on the line. In 1888, volunteer firefighters purchased a plot to bury their deceased brethren. A few years later, a life-sized statue of Robert Brewster, the oldest living fireman at that time, was added. The uniformed statue, weighing 1400 pounds, was sculpted in Italy from Carrara marble, the same material used to create the grieving angels perched on many of Glenwood's tony tombs. Later, a plaque honoring the 23 Texas City firefighters who perished in the 1947 SS *Grandcamp* explosion that killed almost 600 people, was placed on the grounds.

More recently, Anne McCormick Sullivan of Station 68 was laid to rest after she was killed in 2013, battling a five-alarm motel fire that took the lives of three other firefighters as well. Etched on the back of her granite gravestone is her silhouette in a firefighter's helmet. Etched below it are the words, *Courage has a ponytail.* Visitors have left a small perfume bottle and stones, along with remembrances recorded in a journal kept in a waterproof case.

Address 2525 Washington Avenue, Houston, TX 77007, +1 (713) 864-7886, www.glenwoodcemetery.org, info@glenwoodcemetery.org | Getting there Bus 85 to Washington Avenue & Custus Street | Hours Daily 7am–5:30pm | Tip Nonprofit historic crusaders Preservation Houston give docent-led walking tours of Glenwood Cemetery four times a year, as well as tours featuring the historic neighborhoods where many of the interred resided above ground (www.preservationhouston.org).

37 _ Gordy & Sons Outfitters

Tie one on in the city

True Texan and self-proclaimed "gun man who fishes," Russell Gordy didn't skimp on his second love when creating his outdoor enthusiasts' dream emporium, Gordy & Sons Outfitters. The humble and hardworking Gordy brought a taste of the outdoors to the middle of Houston since his successful career in oil and gas and local real estate development keeps him in the city when he'd rather be out hunting or fishing.

It's obvious that his first love is guns when you walk into the store's prized collection of 225 premier firearms crafted by the world's top gunmakers. They are elegantly displayed in the vault's dark walnut cabinets and guarded behind an 18,000-pound antique door from the South Main Bank.

The store's other showstopper is its outdoor casting pond that looks more like the setting for a garden party than for fishing practice. What makes the 80-foot-long, 40-foot-wide, and 12-foot-deep casting pond so special is that it's one of the biggest in the US, and it's fully-stocked with catfish, blue gills, and bass. The pond is an authentic environment for fly fishing aficionados to test out top-of-the-line reels, rods, and lines to find the ideal fit. The friendly staff members are happy to share their expertise and put together the perfect kit for any fishing scenario, including custom ties from their in-house fly tier. The complimentary selection of adult beverages enjoyed pondside helps too.

The enthusiastic instructors offer expert guidance to newbies or tips for those wanting to fine tune their casting skills. Once a month, the store offers free fly-fishing lessons for women and children to encourage this growing demographic within the sport. The staff will even point you in the direction of popular urban angling spots to test out your skills in the wild, like nearby White Oak Bayou. But you may never want to leave this fishing paradise.

Address 22 Waugh Drive, Houston, TX 77007, +1 (713) 333-3474, www.gordyandsons.com, info@gordyandsons.com | Getting there Bus 85 to Washington Avenue & Yale Street | Hours Tue–Sat 10am–6pm | Tip Take in a production at The Gordy, the home of Houston's Stages Repertory Theatre. The 66,850-square-foot, three-theater venue bears the name of regular patrons and generous donors, Glenda and Russell Gordy (600 Rosine Street, www.thegordy.com).

38__ The Gregory School

Honoring the honor roll

Unity, Strength, Perseverance – these precepts are embedded in pavers forming a pathway to the entrance of the African-American Library at the Gregory School. Each principle is illustrated by a West African symbol – symbols that once appeared in brick-laid patterns on the streets of Freedmen's Town in the early 1900s. Home to formerly enslaved individuals in the post-Emancipation era, Freedmen's Town served as the location for the first public elementary school for Black Americans. Built in 1926, the school was named for Edgar M. Gregory, an abolitionist, Union officer, and assistant commissioner of the Freedmen's Bureau, which assisted newly free residents with legal and property matters.

For almost 60 years, grade-schoolers sat in the classrooms of the red-brick, two-story building. After receiving State Archaeological Landmark status in a historic district on the National Register of Historic Places, the African-American Library at the Gregory School opened in 2009. Now, school kids and adults learn from archival material that's part of the Houston Public Library system.

Take a look at the neighborhood's early days in the Freedmen's Town Gallery, a display of memorabilia donated by residents and their descendants, including the granddaughters of Jack Yates, pastor of Antioch Baptist Church and cofounder of Emancipation Park. Vintage photos show children at play, sorority sisters, happy couples, and family gatherings, all documenting everyday life and the material success enjoyed by the Freedmen's Town community.

Success beyond Freedmen's Town is also celebrated. From the Fifth Ward, there's Barbara Jordan, whose oratorical prowess made an impression during her time as the first Black congresswoman from Texas. Movers and shakers in every field inspire future generations, as evidenced by the notes left behind from visitors full of pride and promise.

Address 1300 Victor Street, Houston, TX 77019, www.houstonlibrary.org | Getting there Bus 32 to West Gray & Matthews Street | Hours Tue & Wed 10am–6pm, Thu noon–8pm, Fri & Sat 10am–5pm | Tip Visit nearby Bethel Park, where the design incorporates the exterior masonry walls from the Bethel Missionary Baptist Church, founded by Jack Yates in 1891 (801 Andrews Street).

39 Gulf Building

An art deco jewel

Dwarfed by loftier, modern neighbors, the Gulf Building no longer dominates the downtown skyline, but its gothic grandeur and art deco details are still on display for those visiting this Main Street business hub. Completed in 1929, the 37-story stepped tower covered in Indiana limestone held the title of the tallest building west of the Mississippi for two years and remained the tallest building in Houston until 1963. Topping the tower was an observation deck with a long-range telescope and an aeronautical beacon to light up the night sky.

Commissioned by local magnate Jesse Jones, the ground-floor banking hall built for his National Bank of Commerce is a showstopper. The vaulted gilt ceiling and skylight soar an impressive 43 feet above the patterned terrazzo floor. Embellished with elaborate friezes, the towering French limestone walls create a stately air for checking one's accounts, which you can still do as a client of JPMorgan Chase, the building's current namesake and banking occupant. Eight frescoes detailing moments in Texas and Houston history, including a futuristic Houston skyline complete with a zeppelin, borders the Main Street lobby entrance. The Travis Street entrance received a decorative upgrade with a massive stained-glass window of the Battle of San Jacinto in 1960.

The largest original tenant, Gulf Oil Corporation, who negotiated naming rights with its lease, added its own flair to the building in 1965. A slowly rotating 53-foot neon disc of the Gulf Oil logo replaced the observation tower. When the 1970s energy crisis deemed the electricity powering the 7,350 feet of neon tube excessive, "the lollipop" was removed. Sakowitz Bros. was the other big-name original occupant filling five floors with upscale fashion. Finn Food Hall now occupies the space, where you can try to spot the store's art deco remnants while enjoying happy hour.

Address 712 Main Street, Houston, TX 77002 | Getting there METRORail to Central Station (Red Line) | Hours Unrestricted from the outside | Tip Reliefs of the self-sharpening oil well drill bit patented by Howard Hughes' father, which was also the source of the eccentric tycoon's fortune, trim the façade of the old Hughes Tool Co. art deco building (5425 Polk Avenue).

40__The H.A.M.
Graffiti museum en plein air

In the industrial East End, a gritty, graffiti-covered warehouse challenges the concept of what constitutes a museum. Reluctant to be labeled as artist or curator, the man behind The Harrisburg Art Museum, aka The H.A.M, is Daniel Anguilu, who started his graffiti life painting trains when it was considered a rebellious, illegal act, not street art. During his day job as a METRORail driver, Anguilu frequently passed an abandoned building. He approached the owner for permission to turn into an unofficial safe haven for local graffiti artists to express themselves freely. That was over a decade ago.

Now recognized as a hub for Houston street art, the garage door canvases are covered in murals by local and international artists. Nothing is permanent. Space is allocated to artists who request it, with the row facing Harrisburg Boulevard commonly reserved for visiting painters who want to leave an artistic, albeit temporary, gift to the city. Wildstyles, the intricate graffiti writing that appears illegible to the untrained eye, are often found in the covered loading bay. The large collaborative murals that decorate the inside of the warehouse, alongside a few sculptures, are occasionally viewable on the weekends, but the hours are subject to the whims of the volunteers and artists.

To promote old-school graffiti culture, The H.A.M. hosts battles, a series of head-to-head competitions where new and seasoned artists paint to be crowned the winner. The fast-paced painting sessions result in pieces that are in contrast in energy and style to the commissioned murals that brighten walls around the city.

The pop-up art markets and car shows that take place in the surrounding parking lot often feature live painting to entertain the crowds. The H.A.M. continues to preserve a space for painters to share their art and skills with the community.

Address 4200 Harrisburg Boulevard, Houston, TX 77011, +1 (713) 961-3877, www.facebook.com/thehamhouston | **Getting there** METRORail to Lockwood / Eastwood (Green & Blue Line) | **Hours** Exterior daily dawn – dusk | **Tip** Social protest muralist Leo Tanguma painted his stunning work *The Rebirth of Our Nationality* in 1974 on the East End's Continental Can Company building. Nearly faded from existence, he worked with street artist Gonzo247 to bring new life to his piece depicting the struggles of the Mexican-American community (5800 Canal Street).

41 HCC Central Campus

Head of the class

Located in the quiet part of Midtown on the edge of the Museum District, Houston Community College's scenic Central Campus rewards the curious visitor with architectural eye candy and local history. Leading to the dominating Doric columns of the San Jacinto Memorial Building, a classical revival and art deco masterwork that would be a welcomed addition to any top tier institution, is a timeline walkway chronicling the building's evolution as home to six different educational institutions over its 100-plus years, briefly including the University of Houston.

Before HCC took up permanent residence, the building was San Jacinto High School from 1926 to 1971. Part of the building's recent $60-million restoration pays tribute to the school and its alumni, whose ranks include Walter Cronkite, with fact-filled placards at the main entrance and an encased showroom of "San Jac" memorabilia on the second floor. A walk around the building's exterior reveals preserved art deco, bas-relief panels, fountains, and decorative flourishes missing from modern high schools, like the large medallions of football, basketball, and track and field athletes bordering the attached gymnasium.

A historical marker out in front of the college's Heinen Theatre, formerly Temple Beth Israel, reminds sightseers of its religious past. In 1925, Texas' oldest Jewish congregation built the temple to accommodate its growing numbers. Designed by a fellow member and prominent architect Joseph Finger, the synagogue's art deco architecture also features Middle Eastern elements, such as the preserved symbols inlaid on the portico.

The new buildings also marry the old. The plain brick rear façade of the Learning HUB blends in with the brick of the temple across the walkway, while the front's top-to-bottom glass reflects the San Jacinto Memorial Building, adding to its dramatic appearance.

Address 1300 Holman Street, Houston, TX 77004, +1 (713) 718-6000, www.hccs.edu/
locations/central-college/central-campus | Getting there Bus 09 to Holman & Austin
Street | Hours See website for hours and events | Tip At the edge of campus is Retrospect
Coffee Bar, a 2018 Good Brick Award recipient from Preservation Houston for turning
the old gas station into a popular neighborhood and student hangout. Walk or bike to get a
discount (3709 La Branch Street, www.retrospectcoffeebar.com).

42 Houston Arboretum

Getting back to our roots

"Hidden gem" tends to be the default description for the Houston Arboretum and Nature Center. However, a more accurate label might be, "hiding in plain sight," since the arboretum is centrally located next to Memorial Park, the city's largest urban green space. Perhaps Houstonians are unwilling to believe nature could coexist so close to the standstill traffic on Loop 610. But once you're inside, the concrete jungle gives way to a canopy of trees, and the city literally gets back to its roots.

Well before the forest bathing trend, the arboretum has lured locals to take a walk on the wild side since 1967. As the conservationist stewards of 155 acres of city land, the arboretum operates as a private, non-profit education facility, its mission to keep the area safe and sound. In contrast to a botanical garden showcasing exotic orchids, the flora here is native.

Field stations inform city slickers about the grassland systems and their accompanying wildflowers and wildlife. The arboretum is on the flight path for migrating birds and monarch butterflies, while armadillos, broad banded water snakes, swamp rabbits, and turtles call it home. Eagle-eyed visitors occasionally witness the resident alligator, affectionately known as the Arbor Gator, lolling in the meadow pond.

Five miles of Mother Nature come in the form of marked trails, including the Ravine Trail that features surprising changes in elevation and topography for a notably flat city. Observe the springtime bounty of color on the Wildflower Trail, while fall delivers sunflowers to the Meadow Trail. A variety of terrains, from savannas to the prairie, demonstrate the diversity of Houston's original natural landscape in a serene setting with areas accessible to people of all abilities. However, leave your bikes and running shoes at home, as these paths are designed for less strenuous hiking to nurture your spirit.

Address 4501 Woodway Drive, Houston, TX 77024, +1 (713) 681-8433,
www.houstonarboretum.org, arbor@houstonarboretum.org | Getting there Bus 20 to
Woodway & Memorial Drive | Hours Daily 7am – dusk | Tip Give thanks to Terry Hershey,
the environmentalist who prevented the paving of Buffalo Bayou, when you visit her
namesake park, which runs along the waterway she protected in its natural state for future
generations (15200 Memorial Drive, www.pct3.com/Parks/terry-hershey-park).

43___Houston Dairymaids

Texan curds and whey

You won't find Holstein cows grazing on Airline Drive, a road pop-
ulated by produce wholesalers, *pan dulce* purveyors, and piñata shops.
However, Redneck Cheddar from Veldhuizen Farms in Dublin, Texas,
or Paula Lambert's mozzarella, handmade in her Dallas factory, might
be one of the seven cheeses sampled daily at Houston Dairymaids.
While Dairymaids shows favoritism towards Texas-made cheeses,
cheese-making powerhouses like Vermont and Wisconsin are in the
mix, along with a few European imports. The free cheese tastings
allow for a one-on-one exchange with a Dairymaids cheese monger,
who acts as the spokesperson for the artisan cheesemakers. In a state
where people generally ask, "Where's the beef?" that dairy dialog goes
a long way towards educating consumers that there's more to Texas
than BBQ.

Owner and founder Lindsey Schechter first started with a farmers market stand, where local chefs quickly became customers. That
loyal fan base led to Schechter's role as a wholesaler. She now supplies
over 300 restaurants in Houston and Austin, many of whom proudly
credit Houston Dairymaids on their menus. Obviously, there's more
than the select seven cheeses on the tasting menu available to retail
customers. Parmesan wheels weigh in at 90 pounds, the heaviest carried inside by Dairymaids themselves, as the small storefront has no
loading dock. Over 150 cheese varieties from cow, goat, and sheep
milk are in stock. Cheese plate prerequisites like fresh bread, fruit
conserves, olives, salami, and wine are also for sale.

So why seven tastings instead of the typical "more is more" display of cheeses stacked high in glass cases? Schechter explains the
smaller offering removes the burden of choice, which can overwhelm
and even intimidate customers who might not know where to begin.
But once they do, even goat feta first-timers become part of the
cheese-loving herd.

Address 2201 Airline Drive, Houston, TX 77009, +1 (713) 880-4800, www.houstondairymaids.com | **Getting there** Bus 56 to Airline Drive & Adele Street | **Hours** Tue–Fri 10am–6pm, Sat 10am–4pm | **Tip** Purchase hyperlocal honey or host a beehive in your backyard through the Bee2Bee Honey Collective, founded by Nicole Buergers. Visit www.bee2beehoney.com for retail locations, including Houston Dairymaids, as well as their online shop.

44__ The Houston Fed

All about the Benjamins

Cash is king at Houston's Federal Reserve Bank Branch. But don't roll up unless your vehicle is an armored car and you're depositing stacks of bills rather than rolls of quarters. As the Houston outpost for the Dallas Fed, one of the 12 regional reserve banks in the federal reserve system, this bank serves 41 counties in southeast Texas. Houston's customers include 320 banks and credit unions with multiple branches, all ordering cash each week from the branch. Welcome to the banks' bank, with 12.9 million notes deposited and paid out daily.

Opening in 1919, the Houston office had its headquarters downtown, but growing pains and post-9/11 security concerns led to the construction of the bank's current address. The embassy-strength building makes an impression with a two-ton bronze eagle statue staring down motorists and bicyclists along Allen Parkway. Even touring musician David Byrne took notice of what he described as the "weird, almost surreal post-modern edifice." But the bank's architecture harkens back to earlier times and the shotgun homes once populating the area that inspired the architect Michael Graves. He also flanked the building with a design element suggesting a banker's rolltop desk.

Had David Byrne signed up in advance for a free bank tour, he would have learned all of this information and enjoyed a view of the Monsters, Inc.-style, robotic forklifts gliding on a magnetized path to the processing center. A vault cam provides different vantage points of the second-largest vault in the US that rises to the height of a six-story building. Currency handlers behind protective glass manage the screening machines that process 6.7 million notes a day. Counterfeit bills head to the Secret Service, one of the bank's tenants. Unfit bills are shredded and given to visitors in small bits. Don't bother trying to tape them back together.

Address 1801 Allen Parkway, Houston, TX 77019, +1 (713) 483-3000, www.dallasfed.org/houston.aspx | Getting there Bus 40, 41 to West Dallas & Taft Street | Hours See website for tours and public events | Tip Collectors of rare currency, from obsolete Republic of Texas bills to discontinued, high-denomination Federal Reserve notes buy and sell at U.S. Coins and Jewelry, in business since 1985 (8435 Katy Freeway, www.houstoncoins.com).

45 Houston Polo Club

Hockey on a horse

You'd never know the Sport of Kings was in session given the Houston Polo Club's location near the eternal gridlock of Interstate 10. However, the hustle and bustle eventually give way to an equestrian oasis with the largest polo-playing membership in the United States. Founded in 1928, the Houston Polo Club also has bragging rights as Houston's oldest sports franchise.

While polo is often associated with pomp and circumstance, polo watching on the club's Farish Field is more playful than prim. At the start of the match, dueling polo teams consisting of four mounted riders approach the field to the sound of AC/DC's *Thunderstruck*. Still, spectators dress to impress, particularly in the grandstand where ladies don fanciful fascinators and men sport linen suits. Each game provides approximately two hours of powerful ponies and their players wielding mallets in the hopes of hitting the ball across the goal line on a field that's the equivalent of nine football fields. In true Texas fashion, you can get sized for a pair of custom cowboy boots between chukkers, the seven-minute periods of play making up a match.

Novices to polo watchers will have no problem picking up the game, thanks to the announcer, who weaves sports lingo from basketball to billiards to explain the action. Polo is one of the only sports where fans are allowed on the field at halftime for divot stomping to protect the ponies and players – while sipping champagne. The Houston Polo Club hosts two seasons of Sunday matches in the spring and fall, including the final match for the largest women's polo tournament in the world.

For those inspired to saddle up, the club operates an eight-week polo school, open to the public. Two-hour clinics teaching the basics of mallet swinging and proper polo riding are also offered. However, lefties be warned: polo must be played right-handed.

Address 8552 Memorial Drive, Houston, TX 77024, +1 (713) 681-8571, ext 101, www.houstonpoloclub.com | Getting there By car, take Memorial Drive to the West Loop North Service Road leading to the private drive of the club's entrance | Hours See website for the Sunday polo schedule | Tip Reward the hardworking horses belonging to the Houston Police Mounted Patrol with a carrot or apple at their barn (5005 Little York Road, www.houstontx.gov/police/mounted/visitors.htm).

46 Houston Towers Inn
The ultimate fixer-upper

Against the advice of his realtor, Charles Fondow purchased the dilapidated property at 2309 Wichita Street in 1980 for $35,000. He immediately started restoring the interior, which had previously been turned into a duplex and a daycare before sitting vacant, except for some busy termites, for several years. When a tree crashed through the roof during Hurricane Alicia in 1983, Fondow decided to add a third floor, but, he wondered, why stop there? His skyward architectural dream took flight with a pair of turrets, the beginning of his evolving urban château. A grand contrast to the neighboring two-story brick homes on the block.

A nurse by trade with zero carpentry or major renovation experience, Fondow undertook all the work himself, only hiring a few contractors to assist with his grand design that was inspired by sights from his extensive travels, like Russian onion domes, a Wisconsin courthouse, and a Queens subway stop. A structural engineer would come by to check on his slow progress every six months. Fondow lived for 31 years in his incomplete dream home, always adding to his vision: terraces, an atrium, even an elevator. Sadly, he fell deathly ill on a Caribbean cruise in 2011 and never completed his passion project.

After Fondow's death, the property once again stood empty until real estate developer Nick Urgarov snatched it up at auction in 2014 with the intent to flip it. However, upon learning of Fondow's story, Urgarov felt compelled to carry on his ambitious construction and enhance it with complementary designs to create a boutique hotel. It was an impressive feat, considering Fondow's unconventional engineering. Guests of Houston Towers Inn now enjoy Fondow's millwork, carpentry, and architectural design, complete with luxury details, museum-worthy art collection, and a 360-degree view of the city from one of Fondow's observation decks.

Address 2309 Wichita Street, Houston, TX 77004, +1 (713) 900-7007, www.houstontowers.com, stay@houstontowers.com | Getting there Bus 05 to Southmore Boulevard & South Freeway Service Road | Hours Unrestricted from the outside only | Tip Fondow was very friendly with his neighbors, including Earl Nash, who runs the shoeshine and repair shop across the street (5106 Emancipation Avenue, www.mistershines.com).

47 Ima Hogg's Gardens

Green goddess among the beautiful flowers

Despite Ima Hogg's unflattering name, the woman known as the First Lady of Texas did not reside in anything resembling a pigsty. As a young girl, she lived in the Governor's Mansion, while her father served two terms as the state's first native-born governor from 1891 to 1895. In adulthood, Ima and her two brothers built an estate on 14 acres bordered by Buffalo Bayou. Naming their homestead Bayou Bend for the waterway's curve along the property, the three siblings lived under the same roof, designed by John Staub, architect to Houston's elite, in 1926 (see ch. 12).

Decorating the interior with American antiques, Ima also tackled Bayou Bend's unruly exterior. Faced with a tangly thicket, Ima made a silk purse out of a sow's ear, creating a Southern take on the Gardens of Versailles. Magnolias and crepe myrtles provided much of the Deep South scenery, planted at the request of her brother, Will. After he passed away and her other brother married, Ima became the sole resident in 1930. Like a green-thumbed Diana, the goddess of the hunt who inspired one of the gardens, Ima tracked down flowering species, including a rare camellia from Avery Island, an area better known for tabasco production. Working alongside landscape architects, Ima created nine garden rooms with their own thematic flair, from a butterfly laid out in brickwork and filled in with flowers to the Clio Garden, where boxwood hedges surround a statue of the muse of history.

Most importantly, Ima introduced azaleas to Houston. In spring, a blooming palette of pastels runs throughout Bayou Bend, where azaleas also appear brilliant white in White Garden, which Ima dedicated to Alvin Wheeler, her gardener for 30 years. The gardens, which opened to the public in 1966, are a featured spot on the annual Azalea Trail, organized by the River Oaks Garden Club, which has supervised the gardens since the 1960s.

Address 6003 Memorial Drive, Houston, TX 77007, +1 (713) 639-7750, www.mfah.org/visit/bayou-bend-collection-and-gardens | Getting there Bus 20 to Memorial Drive & Birdsall Street | Hours Tue–Sat 10am–5pm, Sun 1–5pm | Tip The Houston Symphony, co-founded by Ima Hogg, holds an annual, multi-instrument competition named in her honor to support budding musicians (houstonsymphony.org/community/young/ima-hogg-competition).

48 Islamic Da'Wah Center

A spiritual investment

Hakeem "The Dream" Olajuwon earned his nickname thanks to his sublime dunking skills as a member of University of Houston's "Phi Slama Jama" basketball team in the early 1980s. As the star center for the Houston Rockets, his fancy footwork, known as the Dream Shake, propelled the team to successive NBA championships in 1994 and 1995. The MVP also made history as one of the first practicing Muslims in the league. Even while fasting during Ramadan, Olajuwon's basketball prowess never faltered – some opponents remarked that his performance improved during the month-long religious observance.

The Hall of Famer made history again when he founded the city's first downtown mosque in a former bank built in 1928. Olajuwon, a savvy real estate investor, was invited to bid on the building, which had sat vacant for decades. With dramatic bronze doors and neo-classical trimmings, the place already resembled a temple. But it was the ornate domed ceiling that sealed the deal for Olajuwon, who admired the Renaissance-inspired design featuring a Texas lone star in the center. The center opened its doors in 2002.

Friday prayers are for the faithful, many of whom drive in from distant suburbs for the welcoming atmosphere in a space reminiscent of the grand mosques found around the world. Artifacts are on display upstairs, including two framed squares of gold-embroidered cloth that were once draped over the sacred shrine at Mecca. The stately library holds approximately 100,000 books in its collection, in addition to a basketball signed by Olajuwon – the only nod to his time on the court. In keeping with the *da'wah* mission to teach the community about Islam, the center offers lectures and courses taught by noted scholars. Take a tour, suitable for everyone from senior groups to school kids. And don't miss the gift shop that's housed in the former bank's vault.

Address 201 Travis Street, Houston, TX 77002, +1 (713) 223-3311, islamicdawahcenter.org, info@islamicdawahcenter.org | Getting there METRORail to Preston (Red Line) | Hours By tour only, reservation required | Tip If you've got game, show off your crossover dribble at the Fonde Recreation Center, where aspiring b-ballers practice. There's also a Hall of Fame to motivate those with hoop dreams (110 Sabine Street, www.houstontx.gov/parks/communitycenters/cc-fonde.html).

49 Jefferson Davis Hospital

Substratum of spirits

All the makings of a ghost story can be found on a historical marker planted next to a red brick building with a steep stairway that leads to a set of imposing Ionic columns. Etched above those architectural embellishments are the words *Jefferson Davis Hospital*: the city's first public hospital which opened in 1924. However, as the marker explains, the hospital's staff weren't the first inhabitants on this plot of land.

The original occupants were Civil War veterans, former slaves, and victims of yellow fever, all laid to rest in what was the city's first publicly-owned cemetery, in operation from 1840 to 1880. To accommodate the long-term residents, the hospital's basement was built above ground so as not to disturb the graves, which remained on site. Lobbying by Confederate veterans and families resulted in the naming of the hospital after the sole President of the Confederate States of America.

The hospital stayed on this site for 13 years before moving to an updated facility. But in that time span, tales spread of angry ghosts who were no longer resting in peace. Subsequent tenants included a psychiatric facility, juvenile detention ward, and Cenikor, a drug rehabilitation clinic that paid $1 a year for rent in 1973.

In the 1980s, the building sat vacant, tempting paranormal peeping Toms and vandals, who enhanced the haunted vibe with graffiti shout-outs to Satan. However, the historic landmark was rescued from ruin when a partnership between two non-profits, preservation-minded Avenue, and Artspace, an affordable housing advocate for artists, led to the building's restoration in 2005.

Now, creative energy fills the 34 apartments in the building's present incarnation as the Elder Street Artist Lofts. Instead of ghost hunters, art lovers visit the open studios during the yearly Artcrawl held in November. And the angry spirits have settled down – for now.

Address 1101 Elder Street, Houston, TX 77007, www.elderstreetartists.com, www.artcrawlhouston.com | **Getting there** By car, go north on Houston Avenue, turn right on Dart Street, and turn right on Elder Street | **Hours** Unrestricted from the outside only | **Tip** Hardy and Nance Studios in Downtown's Warehouse District is a participating Artcrawl space that also hosts open studios on the third Saturday of each month (902 Hardy Street, www.hardyandnancestudios.com).

50 Johnny Dang & Co.

It don't mean a thing if it ain't got that bling

Statement jewelry takes on a new meaning when you're shopping at Johnny Dang's blingy boutique. His tailormade "grillz," bejeweled mouth pieces covering the teeth like a shimmery suit of armor, are the must-have accessory among Houston's hip-hop and rap intelligentsia, including Johnny's business partner and local rapper Paul Wall. Athletes also order ornamental cap-work here, and all celebrity clients have their dental impressions made in the VIP room. The Houston Astros were fitted with World Series grills after their 2017 win.

You too can customize a wearable work of art. From modest starter grills capping a row of six teeth in gold to Johnny's signature invisible-set diamond grills, the design options are vast. Experienced artisans fulfill orders using specialized equipment and precision tools on-site where the teeth molds of Beyoncé, a Houston native, and hubby Jay-Z are housed in tiny vaults labeled with their likenesses.

Johnny Dang's 14,000-square-foot, sparkly showroom is the largest of its kind. And he offers more than just bespoke grills. Display cases shimmer with rings and watches with a "go big or go home" allure. Charms and pendants celebrate Houston culture from sports teams to slabs – cars with candy paint jobs and shiny, spoked rims, the automobile equivalent of grills. Johnny's wife Jennifer has her own designs, featuring pet ID tags tricked out in precious stones.

Houston's Vietnamese population is the third largest in the country, and Johnny and Jennifer Dang are prominent members of the community. Lunar New Year celebrations complete with a dragon dance performed by a local troupe, plus an annual charity crawfish boil are special events hosted by the couple and open to all. It's no wonder that an official city proclamation declared October 22nd "Johnny Dang Day" in recognition of his creative and charitable contributions.

Address 6224 Richmond Avenue, Houston, TX 77057, +1 (713) 777-2026, www.tvjohnny.net | **Getting there** Bus 25 to Richmond Avenue & Greenridge Drive | **Hours** Mon–Fri 10am–6pm | **Tip** Celebrate Houston's slab culture at the Holiday Car Show held in June at 8th Wonder Brewery where their craft brews include a hip-hop series (2202 Dallas Street, www.8thwonder.com).

51 Julia Ideson Building
A literary ghost

Faint violin music coming from the Tudor Gallery and the distinct sound of dog nails clicking along the tile hallways are just a few signs the ghost of Jacob Frank Cramer and Petey, his German shepherd companion, use to alert staff and visitors of their presence inside the Julia Ideson Building. Named after Houston's first head librarian, the building opened in 1926 as the city's first Central Public Library, where Mr. Cramer was employed as the custodian. He spent 10 years living in the basement of the library alongside his dog, taking care of the building and entertaining himself by playing waltzes on his violin – until he was found dead one morning by the librarians arriving at work.

The Julia Ideson Building is now home to the Houston Metropolitan Research Center, a special collections division within the Houston Public Library System dedicated to documenting and preserving the city's history. One of the center's diligent librarians decided to fact check the Cramer tale. As with any good ghost story, a little digging revealed a few embellishments and misremembered details. Jacob Cramer was employed at the library, but as the guardsman/night watchman, not the custodian. His musical instrument was the coronet, not the violin. He died at the hospital, not the library. And, Petey was likely a small mixed mutt, not a large German shepherd.

The discrepancies don't negate the fact that Cramer and Petey still watch over this historic downtown gem of Spanish Renaissance Revival architecture. Keeping their haunting to the original part of the building, they spend eternity exploring the library's collection of antique books and artifacts in the elegant reading room with marble pillars and multicolored flowered ceiling, studying the city's largest collection of WPA murals that decorate stairwells and hallways, and crashing wedding receptions in the Tudor Gallery.

Address 550 McKinney Street, Houston, TX 77002, +1 (832) 393-1662, www.houstonlibrary.org/location/julia-ideson-building | Getting there Bus 40 to McKinney & Smith Street | Hours Tue & Wed 10am–6pm, Thu noon–8pm, Fri & Sat 10am–5pm | Tip Find your family tree in the Clayton Library Center for Genealogical Research, whose collection was initially housed at the Julia Ideson Building before moving to the historic Clayton House in 1968 (5300 Caroline Street, www.houstonlibrary.org).

52 KPFT 90.1 FM
Left of the dial

When KPFT, part of the progressive Pacifica radio brethren, moved to historic Audubon Place in 1975, residents along the grand esplanade must have muttered, "There goes the neighborhood!" The station has an explosive history.

From KPFT's initial broadcast in 1970, the KKK twice destroyed the station's remote transmitter with dynamite in a six-month period. Nevertheless, given the station's new digs once housed an art gallery where Yoko Ono was a featured artist, neighbors were likely unsurprised by the alt-minded occupants who've been broadcasting from the same location for almost 50 years. The location is called Radio Row because so many commercial radio stations were also headquartered there.

Now, only KPFT remains on the block while maintaining indie cred as the city's only listener-supported radio station. Manned by volunteer DJs who play a melting-pot mix from Indo-Asian to Irish, KPFT carries on the Pacifica tradition of launching musical unknowns who later become legends. Both Lyle Lovett and Steve Earle debuted on KPFT's airwaves, and the station itself was a hangout for bands on the road. Willie Nelson napped in the backyard, Frank Zappa chilled in the lobby, and Lucinda Williams shopped at their annual garage sale.

KPFT's talk radio trends the same way by giving the mike to the unknown presenters on topics covering veganism to the African diaspora. The Prison Show even provides a call-in segment so those with loved ones behind bars can communicate via a shout-out. Go on a studio tour and look for the "Shrine to Intolerance," displaying remnants of the demolished transmitter.

Still, not all are fans of the free speech-loving station. In 2007, a drive-by shooting narrowly missed the grandma DJ spinning zydeco. However, the "Mighty 90" powers on with perennial fund drives in the absence of corporate cash – a survivor still striving for peace.

Address 419 Lovett Boulevard, Houston, TX 77006, +1 (713) 526-4000, www.kpft.org |
Getting there Bus 82 to Westheimer Road & Taft Street | Hours Lobby 10am – 6pm; tours
by appointment | Tip Masala Radio (www.masalaradio.com) broadcasts Bollywood hits on
98.7 FM and hosts the largest Holi Festival in the United States every March.

53__Kuhl-Linscomb
Marketplace of ideas

Concept stores conjure visions of high-design *objets d'art* surveilled by staff clad in black with smirks suggesting, "If you have to ask, you can't afford it." Such is not the case at Kuhl-Linscomb, a very Houston take on lifestyle curation where shoppers are offered margaritas and Topo Chico instead of attitude. Helmed by Pam Kuhl-Linscomb and Dan Linscomb, an affable couple with aesthetic aptitude, this retail retreat would likely stand 20 stories tall, based on the numerous departments that range from apothecary to pet apparel. Instead, the layout is a campus of showrooms housed in five buildings occupying two city blocks.

Campus is the operative word as even design students take field trips to the store known for its visual merchandising cachet. It's a maze you won't mind getting lost in – "Unless you're a minimalist," Pam warns. Find your way using a handy map and the owners' collection of antique props that functions as quirky guideposts. Building 5 acts as the flagship, where vintage, metal bellhops welcome customers to the modern-day bazaar. Mid-century buildings marked by bright green numbers across the street fill out the rest of the campus.

Slow shopping is encouraged, along with sampling, whether it's a Bloody Mary mix or face mask. Table arrangements showcase arrays of items, each one an inspiring vignette allowing imaginations to run wild. Who wouldn't want the whimsy of a Napoleon bust candle in their powder room? Or dream of investing $40,000 for a peaceful slumber on a Swedish Hästens mattress, the priciest product in the store.

At the other end of the price point spectrum lies the popular greeting card section, all chosen by the owners who consider it a victory when they hear laughter in the aisles. Gift giving motivates many shoppers, but few leave without an impulse buy of their own, plus gratis gift wrapping, no questions asked.

Address 2424 West Alabama Street, Houston, TX 77098, +1 (713) 526-6000, www.kuhl-linscomb.com, info@kuhl-linscomb.com | **Getting there** Bus 41 to Kirby Drive & West Alabama Street | **Hours** Mon–Fri 10am–6pm, Sat 10am–5pm, Sun 1–5pm | **Tip** Kuhl-Linscomb plans to enlarge its campus with the addition of nearby Penguin Arms, one of the last survivors of Googie architecture, a West Coast genre of 1950s futurism. Arthur Moss created the kooky six-plex featuring an inverted framework accented by terrazzo panels that looks like a swinging singles pad from the Stone Age (2902 Revere Street).

54 La Carafe

Cash only, and you'll see why

Listen for the cha-ching of the nearly 120-year-old brass cash register as the bartender rings up wine and beer orders at the downtown drinking institution, La Carafe. This beauty behind the bar is an original machine from the National Cash Register Company, which made the "incorruptible cashier" invention a standard in retail business in the late 1800s. A light oiling now and then keeps this working antique in tip-top shape, except the $8 button sticks a bit and records as $9, which happens to be the largest sum the register can record at a time. It takes a while to account for big tabs.

Reaching heights of four to five feet, massive pillars of dripped candle wax towering on each side of the register grow over months, even years, as one votive is placed atop another every few hours. The longest-standing candle witnessed almost 853 days (2 years, 4 months) of drinking before toppling over. For patrons who wish to keep a piece of fallen wax as a memento, the bar keeps a list. Just don't get your hopes up, as the list is often misplaced.

Looking around at the yellowed pictures and dusty wall décor, it's easy to mistake La Carafe for the oldest bar in the city. But this beloved watering hole is actually the second-oldest bar housed in Houston's oldest documented commercial building. The first tenant was Kennedy Bakery, which sold hardtack to Confederate soldiers. The building later served as a trading post, stagecoach stopover, drugstore, and hair salon before becoming a bar in the 1950s.

With its storied history and dimly lit atmosphere, the bar is ripe for haunting. A jealous woman in a white gauzy dress allegedly pushes pretty women down the narrow, uneven staircase, while a former bartender can be heard yelling, "Last call!" Although the staff can't corroborate these ghostly encounters, they do leave a single barstool on the floor each night just in case the resident ghost wants a tipple.

Address 813 Congress Street, Houston, TX 77002, +1 (713) 229-9399, www.yelp.com/biz/la-carafe-houston | **Getting there** Bus 20, 32, 48, 82 to Congress & Milam Street | **Hours** Daily 1pm–2am | **Tip** Head over to nearby Warren's Inn, where the mixed drinks are strong and the jukebox is arguably the best in the city – only La Carafe's jukebox as competition (307 Travis Street).

55__Large & Small Curios
Room of wonder at HMNS

In 1599, Italian apothecary and collector of curios, Ferrante Imperato, published *Dell'Historia Naturale*, a catalog of his odd and exotic objects, which included a rendering of his floor-to-ceiling cabinet of curiosities. Over 400 years later, a copy of this print hangs near the entrance of the *Cabinet of Curiosities* exhibit at the Houston Museum of Natural Science (HMNS), which brings to life Imperato's repository of wonder – right down to the upside-down crocodile attached to the ceiling.

The allure of amassing a mishmash of natural marvels, bizarre monstrosities, and anthropological imports from the New World developed into a full-fledged hobby during the Renaissance and hit its peak popularity in the Victorian Age. These private collections, mostly belonging to elite Europeans, are often credited as the precursor to the modern museum. Keeping true to the tradition, HMNS' marvelous assortment of antlers, animal skins, taxidermied carcasses, gems, steampunk gadgets, and other peculiarities wows visitors, inviting them to ponder the unlabeled objects' origins, purposes, and significance. Some items even awaken the imagination, begging the viewer to ponder: Is that a narwhal tusk or a unicorn horn?

Unlike the mega-museum's other fossils, minerals, and natural history artifacts, inquiring minds and hands are welcome to touch and feel many of the room's treasures. Open a drawer to discover artfully displayed moths. Pet the kangaroo pelt hanging on the wall. Spin the giant antique globe.

Up the stakes of your explorations by booking the Sleuths & Secrets after-hours experience. Using clues and objects found throughout the *Cabinet of Curiosities*, this non-claustrophobic, escape room-like game challenges you and your teammates to solve the mystery of whether Imperato was not only an apothecary, but also an accomplished alchemist with curious secrets.

Address 5555 Hermann Park Drive, Houston, TX 77030, +1 (713) 639-4629, www.hmns.org | **Getting there** METRORail to Museum District (Red Line) | **Hours** Daily 9am–5pm | **Tip** HMNS sought the expertise and inventory of the Wilde Collection, the charming yet chilling oddities emporium, in creating the *Cabinet of Curiosities*. Tragically, the shop was the victim of a malicious arson attack in late 2019. But keep an eye out for its phoenix rising from the ashes once again soon (1446 Yale Street, www.facebook.com/ thewildecollection).

56 Last Concert Café
Tex-Mex, brothels, and drum circles

Knock twice on the unmarked red door to be granted entrance to Last Concert Café, located at the edge of Downtown on an inconspicuous and tricky street to find, even with modern navigation. Elena "Mama" Lopez sold all her jewelry at the age of 62 to build her swan song enterprise in 1949, making it the first woman-owned restaurant in Houston post-World War II.

Guests were only admitted after visual approval from Lopez through the small curtained window inset in the door. If the curtain closed, you were out of luck. Those deemed worthy to step inside this speakeasy restaurant enjoyed freshly prepared tortillas alongside a small menu of dishes that Lopez changed daily. The same recipes are still served today, offering diners retro Tex-Mex with cheese enchiladas and crispy tacos that might not be trendy but are always comforting.

A large outdoor stage area was added in the late 1980s to the café's complex of covered patios and dining rooms, which incorporates two late 19th-century residences. Speculation abounds about the details, but it's well known the houses functioned as popular brothels for decades. Whether Lopez was involved or not with the salacious business, a sign by the bathrooms states she certainly benefited from the bordello's prominent clients, as Interstate 10 conspicuously goes around the café instead of through her property as initially planned.

Live music was always part of the Last Concert Café tradition, and even more so today. The venue is a magnet for free spirits who enjoy the laissez-faire attitude toward the fragrant smoke in the air and a jam band-heavy calendar with several long-standing gigs. For 23 years and counting, the band POTROAST hosts a midnight drum circle every Wednesday, where all are welcome to join in with their own drum or LED flow toy. If you arrive empty-handed, grab a hula hoop off the patio fence and start grooving.

Address 1403 Nance Street, Houston, TX 77002, +1 (713) 226-8563, www.lastconcert.com |
Getting there Bus 11 to Rothwell & Richey Street | Hours Tue–Sat 11–2am, Sun
11am–9pm | Tip McGonigel's Mucky Duck, an Irish pub-themed supper club, hosts
Irish sessions every Wednesday, where those with some musical skills can join in for a song
(2425 Norfolk Street, www.mcgonigels.com).

57 Listening Vessels
Whispers in the park

Downtown Houston is home to Discovery Green's 12 acres of all the urban park essentials: green space, splash pads, parkour classes, dog runs, and a bocce court. Instagram-worthy public art is also on display. Colorful blocks camouflage an underground parking entrance, and *Monument au Fantôme*, Jean Dubuffet's towering red, white, and blue sculptures, stumps viewers trying to find hidden objects in its free-form shapes. However, one deceptively simple installation often goes unnoticed by visitors to this busy park sandwiched between two hotels and the massive convention center.

The *Listening Vessels*, composed of two benches framed in Alabama limestone, sit across from each other near the Family Scent Garden, which is filled with fragrant herbs and night-blooming jasmine. But these concave sculptures appeal to the sense of hearing. Designed by artist Doug Hollis, who specializes in sound sculptures, the curved interiors of his *Listening Vessels* act as parabolic reflectors that collect and carry sound waves, allowing your words, even spoken at the volume of a whisper, to travel and be heard in the other vessel 70 feet away.

In contrast to the *Listening Vessels'* subtle charms, most park-goers are preoccupied with the artist's other installation in the park, the *Mist Tree*. Crowds cool off underneath this stainless steel sculpture powered by 80 nozzles of water, which form a cloud of mist accented by sheets of light rain.

Discovery Green, once a posh residential area in the late 1800s, became a pair of parking lots in the 1980s. In 2008, the park opened to the public, thanks to the efforts of civic-minded philanthropists like Maconda Brown O'Connor, a social worker and advocate for children. O'Connor gifted Discovery Green with the *Listening Vessels*, adding amplified whispers to the park's soundscape and creating a real feast for all the senses.

Address 1500 McKinney Street, Houston, TX 77010, +1 (713) 400-7336, www.discoverygreen.com | Getting there METRORail to Convention District (Purple & Green Line) | Hours Daily 6am–11pm | Tip Look out for Discovery Green's furry employees, June and Mars, two cats who keep urban vermin at bay. Park staff trapped the two felines in 2013 and, following a health inspection, they've been patrolling the grounds ever since.

58 Liz Taylor's Powder Room

Tinseltown's Texas tarmac

The most Hollywood hangout in Houston sits behind the runways of Hobby Airport. Old Hollywood to be exact. In 1940, the city's first municipal airport opened, starring Braniff Airways and Eastern Airlines. Houston-born aviator Howard Hughes parked his planes in a private hangar next door. He later sold his Boeing Stratoliner to wildcatter-turned-local-hotelier Glenn McCarthy, who was flying celebrities in for the debut of his Shamrock Hotel downtown. The airport's art deco lobby could easily be mistaken for a movie set, with frequent flyers like Humphrey Bogart, Bob Hope, and the Rat Pack landing in Houston for rounds of golf followed by performances and parties at the storied hotel in its 1950s heyday.

Elizabeth Taylor and her *Giant* co-stars James Dean and Rock Hudson also made an appearance at the airport while waiting for charter flights to the film's location in Marfa. After Taylor complained that her makeup was melting in Houston's unforgiving heat, the ladies' room was outfitted with a vanity, a pink sofa, and a well-placed fan. Those same amenities still remain in use for the women who visit the airport's second act today as the 1940 Air Terminal Museum.

Aviation buffs have a homegrown Smithsonian after a major restoration. Aerophiles added insider information to the objects on display, including a bullet-ridden beacon donated by Hughes to the terminal. Relics from air travel's golden age range from a Continental Airlines champagne coupe to chic uniforms. In the 1928 Carter Airmail Hangar, visitors can walk on a Lockheed Lodestar, sit in a decommissioned flight simulator, and pose next to a World War II-era Cessna Bobcat, nicknamed the "Bamboo Bomber" for its wooden construction. The museum also welcomes planespotters to their parking lot for a panoramic view of arrivals and departures at neighboring Hobby – no boarding pass necessary.

Address 8325 Travelair Street, Houston, TX 77061, +1 (713) 454-1940, www.1940airterminal.org | Getting there By car, from I-45 South, take exit 40B to TX-35 South/Reveille Street; turn left on Neuhaus Street, which ends at Travelair Street | Hours Tue–Sat 10am–5pm, Sun 1–5pm | Tip Planespotters can also get their fix at George Bush Intercontinental Airport in publicly accessible areas that don't require prior authorization (www.houstonspotters.net/resources/airports).

59 Lost Donnellan Crypt

What lies beneath

Houston's origins lie at the banks of Buffalo Bayou, where Augustus Chapman Allen and his younger brother John Kirby Allen founded the city on August 30, 1836. The East Coast real estate duo promoted the health benefits of this emerging Gulf Coast metropolis with advertisements touting the city's "abundance of spring water" and refreshing sea breezes. In reality, Houston's humidity outmatched any alleged cool air, especially in the summer, and the bayou water was undrinkable. The streets were a sludgy mess of earth and water, earning early Houstonians the derisive nickname "mud turtles" for the sorry state of their thoroughfares. Later, in the late 1860s, much of the population perished in a yellow fever epidemic.

However, neither disease nor unsanitary drinking water led to the demise of Henry Donnellan, son of a Houston settler from Ireland. After the Civil War ended, Confederate troops returning home sank ammunition barges and dumped munitions in Buffalo Bayou to prevent their seizure by the Union Army. However, this plan tragically backfired. In 1867, Henry and his business partner A. C. Richer were blown to smithereens while handling unexploded artillery they found in the bayou's shallow waters. A reporter for *The Telegraph* described the gory aftermath as a horrific scene of mutilated limbs, lacerations, and lost fingers.

Henry's remains were placed in the Donnellan's red-bricked family crypt overlooking the same bayou where he drew his last breath. In the early 1900s, the family's remains were transferred to Glenwood Cemetery because the new Franklin Street bridge was being built just above the crypt, making it no longer a suitable resting place. In a city where historic preservation often gives way to development, the face of the unmarked crypt is still visible, with bricks now painted white and planks of weathered wood serving as a doorway to the past.

Address Underneath the Franklin Street bridge (709-715 block), Houston, TX 77002 | **Getting there** Bus 30 to Franklin & Milam Street; at the northwest corner of the Chase Bank parking lot (716 Franklin Street), walk down the stairs underneath the Franklin Street bridge to reach the Buffalo Bayou Hike and Bike Trail. The crypt is visible from the right. | **Hours** Daily dawn–dusk | **Tip** Join the Mud Turtle program at Hay Merchant, a craft beer bar where members compete in blind tastings to win prizes (1100 Westheimer, www.haymerchant.com).

60 Lucky Land

Visit ancient China without getting on an airplane

Ride a rickshaw through Chinese history at Lucky Land, a whimsical theme park located amongst the bustling Hispanic flea markets and *mercados* on Airline Drive. Owner Mrs. Lee created the park after acquiring a replica of the famous Terracotta Army from the now-closed Forbidden Gardens roadside attraction in Katy, a far west suburb on the outskirts of Houston. The 6,000-strong warrior reproductions – one-third the size of the original funerary artwork that guards the tomb of The First Emperor of China – now anchor the interactive exhibits recreating a piece of China in Houston.

In a selfie-obsessed world, Mrs. Lee manages to sneak in an educational overview of the history and customs of her homeland against the picture-perfect backdrops of her thoughtfully curated displays, like the nook with colorful opera masks showcasing symbols from past dynasties. She employs feng shui concepts to create a welcoming and peaceful environment for her passion project.

Guests are supplied with bright paper umbrellas to beat the Texas sun while wandering through Lucky Land's two acres. Start at the popular Panda Village, a two-story display of life-sized, playful panda statues commissioned from pictures Mrs. Lee took on one of her visits to China. Learn the traditional Shaolin Kung Fu stances by posing with the bronze statues demonstrating the postures. For good luck, rub the Buddha belly in the Happy Buddha Sanctuary before taking a break by the serene water features starring custom-made jade fountains.

The park is especially festive during the Chinese New Year to celebrate the start of the lunar calendar and the year's Chinese zodiac animal. Panda-costumed mascots roam through the crowds, who also enjoy Lion and Dragon Dances, martial arts demonstrations, and musical performances. Everyone leaves with a customary red envelope enclosing a gold coin for good fortune.

Address 8625 Airline Drive, Houston, TX 77037, +1 (281) 447-3400, www.facebook.com/
luckylandhouston | Getting there Bus 56 to Airline Drive & Louise Road | Hours Tue–Fri
10am–5pm, Sat & Sun 10am–6pm | Tip The Chinese Community Center offers Asian
Heritage Tours of Houston's Asiatown and Mahatma Gandhi District, plus cooking
workshops and cultural performances (9800 Town Park Drive, www.cchouston.org/tour).

61 Magic Island

Abracadabra – you're back in the 1980s

Sitting in traffic on Houston's Southwest Freeway can seem like an eternity as 9-to-5ers make their workday exodus. And when a massive pharaoh's head suddenly appears, rising from the feeder road like a B.C.-era mirage, you might even believe you're destined to spend the afterlife bumper to bumper. However, this ancient Egyptian ruler, gilded and stoic, is no rush hour apparition. Welcome to Magic Island, a themed supper club straight out of the 1980s, which offered up to six magic shows a night accented by King Tut opulence. Strolling magicians – and even a mummy – entertained diners who capped off their evening in the disco featuring a desert oasis backdrop.

However, no mystery surrounds the club's closure in 2008. Hurricane Ike, in an unfortunate sleight of hand, caused the neon lights circling the building to catch fire. The subsequent water damage forced Magic Island to shut down and cancel standing reservations for the upcoming holiday season. Like many residents faced with rebuilding, the transformation process took longer than expected. Still, the pharaoh remained on watch as curious commuters made their way past the magic club turned modern-day ruin.

Vandals, channeling Egyptian tomb raiders, plundered the display cabinets containing magician memorabilia and even snatched two of the seated pharaoh statues, along with every electrical wire. Still, Magic Island showed no signs of disappearing. Nor did Manny Fahid, the club's general manager who began his career there as a bartender in 1984. With new hieroglyphic-styled murals on the walls, including a room depicting Cleopatra's lavish barge, and the recovery of one of the pharaoh statues, Fahid plans on resuming his role when Magic Island again wows spectators with a lavish reopening scheduled for 2021. Until then, locals can rest assured that Magic Island's comeback is no illusion.

Address 2215 Southwest Freeway, Houston, TX 77098, +1 (713) 526-2442, www.magicislandhtx.com | Getting there Best viewed driving from I-69/US 59 north at exit Greenbriar Drive/Shepherd Drive | Hours Exterior view unrestricted; check website for reopening date | Tip Once regarded as the "Eighth Wonder of the World" by sports fans, the Astrodome sits vacant next to its replacement, NRG Stadium. View the exterior of the first domed stadium on your way to a Houston Texans game or the rodeo (3 NRG Parkway).

62 Market Square Clock
Making up for lost time

Standing 65-feet tall on the corner of Travis and Congress Streets is the Market Square Clock Tower, officially named the Louis and Annie Friedman Clock Tower for the Hungarian immigrant parents of construction worker, Saul Friedman, who paid for it. Wound by hand every eight days, the clock's four faces, each measuring 7.5-feet wide, once again keep time for the city of Houston after a mysterious journey from City Hall to junkyard heap.

The clock's history began across the street in Market Square Park, Houston's original town center, the seat of City Hall, and a busy marketplace for farmers and merchants selling local goods and imports arriving from nearby Allen's Landing. After the third City Hall building in Market Square burned down in 1903 (the previous two also succumbed to fire), the city commissioned the clock for $1,100 from esteemed clockmaker Seth Thomas Clock Company that would adorn the tower of the fourth (and final) building that would serve as City Hall in the same location. The clock stayed there until 1960, when it was removed and packed in a storage crate before the building's demolition.

Forgotten, sold, or stolen – no one knows how the clock ended up for sale in a junkyard. Ignorant of the clock's origin, Clyde E. Gray purchased and restored it for a historic park in Woodville, Texas, roughly 100 miles northeast of the city. Somehow, Houston officials realized the clock was missing and requested its return. With no proper provenance provided during the sale, Gray returned the clock to the city. He was proclaimed an honorary Houstonian for his cooperation.

In 1996, the clock was installed in its current home, along with the 2,800-pound bell that survived the 1903 City Hall fire (and a stay in the city's storage facilities). Once again, these city artifacts resume their prominent spot watching over Houston's historic Market Square.

Address 301 Travis Street, Houston, TX 77002 | Getting there Bus 108, 209, 236, 291 to Travis & Congress Street | Hours Unrestricted | Tip Almost sold by the city, the historic Sweeney Clock was rescued and re-homed to the downtown Theater District, where it sits on a base of 11,000 bricks that once paved Navigation Boulevard (corner of Capitol Street and Bagby Street, www.houstontx.gov/parks/artinparks/sweeneyclock.html).

63 Memo's Record Shop #1
The rhythm is going to get you

One little Latin music store in Houston's East End is holding out against the tide of streaming music. After all, since opening the shop in 1968, Guillermo "Memo" Villareal has seen every phase of aural consumption: LPs, 45s, 8-tracks, cassettes, and CDs. But his passion for music and sharing it with his customers remains the same. Together with Memo Jr., the father and son duo assist customers in navigating the aisles jam-packed with CDs of every Spanish-language genre. For dance music, comb through the salsa, merengue, cumbia, and bachata bins. Delve into the local scene with a La Mafia album. Or, ask a Memo to suggest a classic from the legendary crooner José José.

Proudly displayed using any space available throughout the store are photos and memorabilia from the elder Memo's career as a local and regional promoter. Bring your *abuelos* to fawn over the signed guitar from Juan Gabriel, the Mexican Elton John, who left behind the memento of his first show in Houston, organized by Memo Sr. In a glass case is the magnificent *charro* suit Vicente Fox wore to his sold-out 1975 concert alongside a picture of him gifting it to the then-young promoter. Either of the Memos will happily regale you with stories behind each photo, like when Selena visited the store, or when Memo Sr. accompanied Puerto Rican boy band Menudo, including a fresh-faced Ricky Martin, on their very first US tour.

The original location was across the street where Refresqueria Tampico #1 now stands. In 1979, they moved into the current, canary yellow store built by Memo Sr.'s brother, which still entices customers inside with muralist Eduardo Jaramillo's eye-catching portraits of icons from the "The Golden Age" of Latin music. Neither Memo Sr. nor Jr. have any plans to stop manning their epicenter of Latin music in Houston. As long as there are records to sell, they'll be here.

Address 703 75th Street, Houston, TX 77011, +1 (713) 928-9291 | **Getting there** Bus 20 to Canal & 75th Street | **Hours** Daily 10am–7pm | **Tip** Gianfranco Gabbanelli learned the intricacies of crafting accordions growing up in Italy, the instrument's birthplace. When he immigrated to Houston, he tweaked the instrument to enhance the sound of the Mexican regional music he heard. His colorful works of art can be found at his namesake store now run by his son (4991 West Bellfort Avenue, www.gabbanelli.com).

64 MFAH's Odyssey
An artful explosion

In a two-second flash, *Odyssey* transformed from a public creation into an enduring artwork. The serene scene commissioned in 2010 by the Museum of Fine Arts Houston (MFAH) for its new Arts of China Gallery is the work of gunpowder artist Cai Guo-Qiang. Known for his creative explosions in the sky, Cai's resume includes the firework footprints that marched across the skyline during the opening ceremony of the 2008 Beijing Olympics. On a smaller scale, he harnesses his explosive skills to create pyrotechnic paintings. But this modern Chinese landscape measuring 10 feet tall and 162 feet long was the largest he had ever attempted.

Over three days inside a rented warehouse, 107 local volunteers assisted Cai in preparing the drawing for the igniting reveal. Using a marker and a paintbrush duct-taped to broomsticks, Cai sketched the mountain, coastline, waterfall, scholar's rock, and garden elements that were then carefully traced with box cutters to create the stencil. Under the watchful eye of the Houston Fire Marshal, Cai spread various grades of gunpowder over the stencil. to achieve his desired explosive effects. As volunteers stood by with cotton pom-poms to snuff out any errant flames, Cai calmly used a smoking incense stick to spark the fire that ripped across the canvas with a deafening boom, permanently blasting the image onto the 42 panels.

The piece was installed the next day, and the gallery smelled faintly of firecrackers on the 4th of July. That familiar scent is gone today, no longer providing visitors with a clue that gunpowder was the medium of choice for the painting covering the gallery's walls. Instead, *Odyssey* is often mistaken for a lovely charcoal drawing complementing the displays of floral porcelain, intricate calligraphy, and other delicate objects from the MFAH's Chinese collection calling out for a closer inspection.

Address 1001 Bissonnet, Houston, TX 77005, +1 (713) 639-7300, www.mfah.org, guestservices@mfah.org | Getting there METRORail to Museum District (Red Line) | Hours Wed 11am–5pm, Thu 11am–9pm, Fri & Sat 11am–6pm, Sun 12:30–6pm | Tip Exiting into the Arts of India Gallery, walk over to the locked glass doors, where you'll be looking out the museum's original neoclassical entrance built in 1924. Head to the South Lawn where you can also see the flashy *Albero Folgorato* (Lightning Tree) sculpture up close.

65 Moody Park

Panic in the park

Unlike the bronze statue of stoic Sam Houston astride his horse in Hermann Park, *Vaquero*, overlooking Moody Park, depicts a Mexican cowboy riding a bucking bronco painted a glossy, royal blue. The artist, Texas native Luis Jimenez, created the 16-foot, fiberglass-on-steel sculpture in 1980. Four versions of *Vaquero* exist, along with an artist's proof, which stands at the entrance of the Smithsonian American Art Museum as the esteemed collection's unofficial symbol. Houston's version, commissioned as a work of public art, pays tribute to the Northside neighborhood's Hispanic heritage with a figure honoring the master horsemen of the American Southwest. The artist, in a horrific twist of fate, died in 2006 while working in his studio – impaled by his own sculpture, a 32-foot-tall mustang.

The colorful exuberance of *Vaquero* is tempered by Moody Park's tragic history as the scene of the city's worst riot. In 1977, Jose Campos Torres, a young Hispanic Vietnam veteran was arrested for a barroom brawl. Police officers savagely beat Torres and pushed him into Buffalo Bayou, where his lifeless body washed ashore on Mother's Day.

Compounding the tragedy, lenient sentences for the officers, amounting to one-year probation and a $1 fine, were handed down. Community outrage culminated in a violent clash between Cinco de Mayo revelers and police officers responding to a disturbance report in Moody Park. The party-turned-police-protest unfolded on Walter Cronkite's CBS evening broadcast, with scenes of anger, massive arrests, and property destruction.

Since 2016, the Torres family has led a march on Cinco de Mayo, retracing the final hours of their loved one's life as a reminder of the ongoing fight against police brutality. Moody Park is now the scene of family gatherings, soccer games, a community pool, and the gun-slinging *Vaquero* in the middle of it all.

Address 3725 Fulton Street, Houston, TX 77009, +1 (713) 692-6925, www.houstontx.gov/parks/artinparks/vaquero.html | Getting there METRORail to Moody Park (Red Line) | Hours Daily dawn–dusk | Tip Houston's Mini Murals project transforms utility boxes into works of art. Self-taught painter Anat Ronen reimagined the metal canvas as a piece of Mexican Talavera tile that brightens up a corner a few blocks from Moody Park (corner of Fulton and Bigelow Streets, www.minimurals.org/murals/fulton-bigelow).

66__Mount Rush Hour
Highway head turner

A Texas twist on Mount Rushmore greets thousands of commuters every day along the Interstate 10 and Interstate 45 interchange. The tiny American Statesmanship Park is home to the oversized busts of George Washington, Abraham Lincoln, Sam Houston (the city's namesake and 1st and 3rd President of the Republic of Texas), and Stephen F. Austin (known as the founder of Texas). The four 16-foot-tall sculptures are secured atop a six-foot black base emblazoned with the words, *A Tribute to American Statesmanship*, creating *Mount Rush Hour*, a work by David Adickes, a local sculptor in his nineties.

Known for his larger-than-life figures, Adickes' first large-scale presidential project also stands roadside along Interstate 45, just 65 miles north of Houston in Huntsville, Texas, where he was commissioned to create a giant Sam Houston. Unsure of how tall to make the statue, he recalled a book from his childhood, *Six Feet Six, The Heroic Story of Sam Houston*, referring to Houston's height and decided to make him 10 times as tall: 65 feet. From then on, Adickes scaled his works by 10. Using old photographs and paintings for models of his historical figures, his real challenge with *Mount Rush Hour* was creating the back of the heads, since there's no evidence of what they looked like.

Finding the park can be a challenge, as it's tucked away on an awkward block in the First Ward formerly occupied by a small Baptist church destroyed in a flood. You can still walk around the church's visible foundation where *July 9th 1970* is inscribed on the southwest corner and two sets of three steps remain of the entrance. Other than the newer townhomes built no more than 12 feet away from the sculpture's base, giving the homeowners an interesting view, there's not much to the park, making *Mount Rush Hour* a true Houston landmark, as it is best viewed speeding down the interstate.

STATESMANSHIP

Address 1400 Elder Street, Houston, TX 77007 | Getting there Bus 44 to Houston Avenue & Bingham Street | Hours Unrestricted view from Interstate 10 | Tip Adickes counseled artist Mai Chi as she created her 72-foot-tall statue of Quan Âm, Goddess of Mercy, who watches over a pond in the serene grounds of the Vietnamese Buddhist Center in the Houston suburb of Sugar Land (10002 Synott Road, Sugar Land, www.vnbc.org/TTPG/ Buddhist_new.aspx).

67 Neon Boots
No standing or drinks on the dance floor

Come ready to dance – and preferably dressed for the part in a pair of boots and Wranglers, when you show up at Neon Boots Dancehall & Saloon. The largest country-themed LGBTQ+ bar in the Lone Star State opened its doors in 2013, when the owners found themselves without a two-steppin' home because the last rainbow-proud honkytonk in Montrose, Houston's historically gay neighborhood, closed its doors earlier that same year.

Breathing new country-and-western life into the space that once housed the legendary Esquire Ballroom, a country music venue from 1955 to 1995, the bar's friendly regulars are quick to introduce newbies to the original white oak dance floor. Amateurs from all walks of life benefit from the weekly complimentary dance lessons from the Neon Mavericks, professional dancers who teach two-step, line dances, and West Coast swing. Illuminating the dance floor in sparkling light is a pair of mirrored disco boots that were co-owner Debbie Storrs' first-ever pair she danced in until they had holes. The dance hall is still home to the stage that hosted country music legends like Loretta Lynn, Kenny Rogers, Dolly Parton, and Waylon Jennings during the Esquire's 40-year run. Even a young, cash-strapped Willie Nelson was given a spot in the house band after its leader refused to buy Willie's songs for $10 each and advised Nelson to hold on to the songs because they were too good. Allegedly, one of those songs was *Crazy*, which would be a hit for Patsy Cline, who performed on the same stage. The Esquire Room, a small bar chronicling the history of the venue's bygone era, is where you can take a break from boot-scooting and take a turn at karaoke.

If dancing isn't your thing, this reinvented roadhouse hangs up its boots for a few hours to host a variety of special events like bingo nights, drag pageants, and Twister competitions in the spacious outdoor patio.

Address 11410 Hempstead Road, Houston, TX 77092, +1 (713) 677-0828, www.neonbootsclub.com | Getting there Bus 85 to Antoine Drive & Mitchelldale Street | Hours Wed & Thu 4pm–midnight, Fri 4pm–3am, Sat noon–2am, Sun noon–midnight | Tip Hunt for honkytonk accessories at Thompson's Antique Center of Texas where you can find vintage cowboy boots, retro western wear, and maybe a Patsy Cline album in this massive mall of antiques and collectibles (9950 Hempstead Road, Unit 600, www.antiquecenteroftexas.com).

68 Numbers Nightclub
Music nonstop through the decades

When Morrisey, moody front man of The Smiths, canceled on Houston fans for the third time, Numbers offered drink specials. When David Bowie passed away, Numbers' annual birthday bash for the club's unofficial patron saint provided the soundtrack for mourners to dance the blues away underneath a giant lightning bolt. For over 40 years, Numbers has given shelter to city kids and suburban outcasts from the Reagan era, the emo-infused 1990s, and now millennials. Whoever comes here today inevitably asks the question, "Why is that club called 'Hashtags'?"

While the younger generation can't relive the Montrose neighborhood of yesteryear, when the lower Westheimer strip was a runway for drag queens, mohawks, and Hare Krishnas, Numbers is a gateway to the past. As one of the oldest continually operating alternative music venues in the country, Numbers eschewed club scene trends in favor of a simple formula: two disco balls, a fog machine, and music spun by resident Numbers DJ, Wes Wallace. Classic Numbers, the city's longest running Friday night dance party, offers a groove of 1980s new wave, electronica, and indie sounds that's far from routine. Nothing is pre-programmed, except a guarantee that Wallace will likely honor recurring requests for Depeche Mode and New Order with his custom remixes and videos providing visual stimulation on the club's big screens.

The club's concrete bunker exterior hasn't changed much either, except for a mural of 1980s music greats, including Debbie Harry, Robert Smith of The Cure, Siouxsie Sioux, Joey Ramone, and Kraftwerk, that receives salutes from patrons heading inside. Although live performances are less frequent on the stage graced by both Grace Jones and Nine Inch Nails, the spotlight occasionally shines on a marriage proposal for a couple who will hopefully live happily ever after, or at least as long as Numbers is around.

Address 300 Westheimer, Houston, TX 77006, +1 (713) 521-1121,
www.numbersnightclub.com | Getting there Bus 82 to Westheimer Road & Taft Street |
Hours Doors open Friday at 9pm for Classic Numbers; see website for event calendar | Tip
Club kids of all ages congregate 24/7 at House of Pies for diner breakfasts, milkshakes, and
a slice of pie à la mode (3112 Kirby Drive, www.houseofpies.com).

69 __ Odd Fellows Lodge #225

Where the odds are in your favor

What did FDR and P. T. Barnum have in common? Both the states-man and the showman belonged to the Independent Order of Odd Fellows (IOOF). The fraternal organization with the funny name began in 18th-century England before traveling across the pond to Baltimore, where the first American lodge was established in 1819. The first Texas Odd Fellows called Houston home with a lodge named Lone Star #1, established in 1838. Now, Houston members meet at Lodge #225, chartered in 1905, in the historic Heights neighborhood.

Unlike the Masons with their secret high society standing, Odd Fellows often live up to their name with a demographic that's heavy on artists and musicians. Jam sessions and art cars are common sights at their annual Chili Cook Off and Sausagefest fundraisers, where the public can mingle with members. The Odd Fellows also host a monthly open house featuring a fridge full of beer and a guided tour for the curious. Along with displays of memorabilia, guests head upstairs to the meeting room draped in silk banners depicting mystic symbols, some whose meanings are only known to members. Visitors learn quickly that positivity, not politics, underlies the IOOF credo represented by the triple links of Friendship, Love, and Truth. The only election talk permitted here concerns lodge positions. The highest ranking office, Noble Grand, is currently held by a woman.

No matter the degree reached or regalia worn, all members act as a safety net for each other and the community at large. The Houston chapter assists the caretakers at Olivewood, the city's first incorporated Black cemetery, with restoration and maintenance. Once a month, members clean headstones and mow the grounds, which include the final resting place of several Odd Fellows, many of whom bear the three-link chain symbol on their headstones – representing a bond formed for eternity.

Address 115 East 14th Street, Houston, TX 77008, www.houstonheightslodge225.com | **Getting there** Bus 40 to Heights Boulevard & East 14th Street | **Hours** Open house on the first Tuesday of every month at 7:30pm; check website for annual events | **Tip** You don't have to be a *sensei* to sit in meditation at the Houston Zen Center, which offers a free class on the first Wednesday of the month at 6:30pm (1605 Heights Boulevard, www.houstonzen.org).

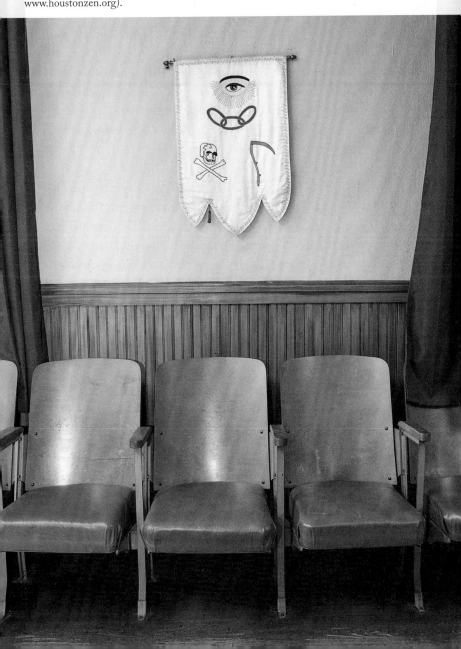

70__ The Old Cotton Exchange

Sitting high in cotton

Before oil and gas was Houston's economic powerhouse, there was cotton. Used to create textiles, cooking oil, and even the first version of plastic, this major cash crop was the catalyst for much of the city's early infrastructure, from a bustling port to well-connected railroads. The wealthy cotton merchants not only lobbied for these facilities, but also served as Houston's first bank, using cotton as loan collateral, as banking was illegal in Texas before the Civil War. Founded in 1874, the Houston Cotton Exchange and Board of Trade oversaw Houston's voluminous trade, which was one of the largest cotton markets in the world, exporting crops as far as Japan.

Needing a grand space to conduct their business, the association commissioned local architect Eugene Heiner, a prominent designer of county courthouses and jails, to build their three-story headquarters, conveniently located downtown in between Market Square and Allen's Landing. Renowned for its Renaissance Revival architecture, the resulting red-brick building, completed in 1884, now stands four-stories tall, as a top floor was added during a 1907 remodel. The exterior's decorative touches include a round arch entrance, contrasting stonework, and four angels carved into the façade, Heiner's tribute to his four daughters. In 1924, the growing exchange moved its operations to a new building, which still bears its name at 1300 Prairie Street.

Today, instead of cotton commodities, contracts and court proceedings are the topics of discussion amongst the lawyers and bail bond agents occupying the listed historical building's office suites. The original ornate trading room was recently home to Public Services Wine & Whisky, until the popular bar closed in November 2020, another victim of the pandemic, leaving only the cherubs adorning the preserved Victorian interior to watch over this historic space for now.

Address 202 Travis Street, Houston, TX 77002 | **Getting there** Bus 265, 269 to Franklin & Travis Street | **Hours** Unrestricted from the outside | **Tip** Heiner also designed the W. L. Foley Building, which is just a few doors down on the same block. It is now home to a gastro lounge, Hearsay, which incorporates Heiner's architectural details into its décor and vibe (218 Travis Street, www.hearsaygastrolounge.com).

71__The Orange Show

Step up for the grand citrus sideshow

Postal worker Jeff McKissack dedicated 24 years of his life to building a funky monument to his favorite citrus fruit, the orange, in the middle of a blue-collar neighborhood. Developing his passion for the orange (the whole fruit, not the juice) while hauling citrus all over the South during the Depression, he continued to devise his treatise on the fruit's virtues over the years. So in 1956, it made perfect sense to him to construct his fruity masterpiece covering 3,000 square feet on the plot of his failed greenhouse and nursery.

McKissack's obsession comes to life in an architectural maze of enclosed rooms, open-air walkways, arenas, and rooftop observation decks all created from items found along his mail route and his excursions to junkyards and antique shops. Only a visionary folk artist like McKissack could put all the pieces together. Wagon wheels, statuary, and scrap-metal birds adorn the walls of his fortlike structure. Eighty cast-iron tractor seats surround the concert stage. Tiled signs of Confucius aphorisms and frog fables preach to visitors. And a disturbing display in a dark, narrow room features nightmare-inducing clowns and a doll-like mannequin dressed as a bride, representing the purity of the orange.

Although McKissack was certain The Orange Show, his obscure monument to the vitamin C-rich fruit, would be a bigger tourist attraction than the Astrodome, the crowds never came when it opened to the public on May 9, 1979. Sadly, a few months later he died of a stroke.

However, his iconic sideshow was appreciated by 21 art-loving Houstonians, including members of ZZ Top and a funeral director, who formed The Orange Show Center for Visionary Art to purchase and preserve the attraction. The organization is now the custodian of Houston's outsider art landmarks and organizer of the legendary annual Art Car Parade (see ch. 6).

Address 2401 Munger Street, Houston, TX 77023, +1 (713) 926-6368, www.orangeshow.org |
Getting there By car, Interstate 45 southbound to exit 43A Telephone Road | Hours See
website for seasonal hours, closed Dec–Feb | Tip In the spirit of The Orange Show, the
adjacent lot has been transformed into Smither Park, where over 300 artists have contributed
to the sparkly mosaics decorating the walls, amphitheater, and pavilion (2441 Munger Street,
www.orangeshow.org/smither-park).

72_Original Kolache Shoppe
Czech out this bakery

Since it was first introduced to Texas in the late 19th century by Czech immigrants, the kolache has earned a spot as a state delicacy alongside other eminent food traditions like BBQ and breakfast tacos. The Original Kolache Shoppe, the oldest Czech bakery in Houston, serves one of the finest versions of this open-faced pastry, marked by the slightly-sweet, slightly-yeasty, pillowy dough filled with fruit, poppy seed, or sometimes fresh farm cheese, and topped with *posipka*, a buttery crumb topping.

Lorraine Sharp started the small, family-run bakery in 1956 using recipes passed down to her from the "Old Country." Continuing the baking legacy is third-generation owner Kevin Dowd, who employs the same old-school methods honed by his mother and grandmother to supply a constant stream of hot, fresh-baked kolaches, *klobasneks* (kolache's sausage cousin), cinnamon rolls, and turnovers every day to a continuous flow of customers.

The inside of the tiny cottage on Telephone Road still feels like you're walking into a grandma's inner sanctum, even with a bit of sprucing up in the past few years. New menu items reflect the changing tastes and diversity of Houston, like the "croissants," hand pies made from a phyllo-like dough with hearty fillings featuring applewood smoked bacon and Tex-Mex flavors. Sister company Zeppelin Coffee now serves quality artisan roasts and lattes to pair with the sweet and savory treats in the bakery case.

A short distance from Hobby Airport, The Original Kolache Shoppe is often the first or last stop in the city for fans. A group of dedicated car lovers gather on-site and in surrounding parking lots for Cars and Kolaches meet-ups on select Sundays throughout the year. Even though Dowd claims, "No one *needs* to eat a kolache," the 64-year-old bakery's loyal following, many of whom are considered family, would disagree.

Address 5404 Telephone Road, Houston, TX 77087, +1 (713) 649-0711, www.originalkolache.com | **Getting there** Bus 40 to Telephone Road & Park Place Boulevard | **Hours** Mon–Sat 5am–noon, Sun 6am–1pm | **Tip** Arrive early to beat the line out the door for the Texas-sized portions at Tel-Wink Grill, a traditional diner on Telephone Road whose menu hasn't changed much since it opened in 1952 (4318 Telephone Road, www.tel-wink.com).

73 PABA

Home of Houston's first fighting preacher

Houstonians filled the Astrodome to watch the legendary Muhammad Ali take down Cleveland "Big Cat" Williams, Ernie Terrell, Jimmy Ellis, and Buster Mathis in high-profile fights. However, it was at the Astrohall during the "sparring match of the century" on July 23, 1971, that Houston's own Rev. Ray Martin knocked The Greatest to the mat not once, but twice. Threatening to "send the fighting preacher to heaven in round seven," Ali got his rematch later that year at the Progressive Amateur Boxing Association (PABA) where the good Reverend sent Ali to the mat for the third time.

During the years surrounding Ali's 1967 Houston trial and conviction for being a conscientious objector to the draft, he lived on and off in the Third Ward. He came to know Rev. Ray Martin, who started PABA in the neighborhood in 1968, adopting the motto, "You Can't Open a Knife or Fire a Gun with a Boxing Glove On!" Ali would pop into the boxing gym and community organization to encourage the area's youngsters who were learning not only boxing skills, but also life skills like discipline, character, and commitment to help them succeed outside the ring.

The gym's floor-to-ceiling showcase proudly displays the trophies, awards, and achievements of PABA athletes and coaches. Visitors can peruse the walls and office windows covered in old newspaper clippings and pictures of Rev. Martin with famous boxers, presidents, and local celebrities, like Marvin Zindler. However, the memorabilia represents only a small portion of Rev. Martin's notable career as a boxer, civil rights activist, and youth advocate. Now in his 80s, the Reverend has turned over the day-to-day operations of PABA to his son, Ray Martin, Jr. But he still stops in a few evenings a week when the gym comes alive with boxers of all ages and skill levels jumping rope, hitting the bags, and sparring in the ring where Ali was felled.

Address 3212 Emancipation Avenue, Houston, TX 77004, +1 (713) 520-9585, www.facebook.com/OfficialProgressiveAmateurBoxingAssociation | Getting there Bus 09 to Emancipation Avenue & Francis Street | Hours Mon–Fri 3–9pm, Sun 2–5pm | Tip Take a lap around nearby Emancipation Park, the oldest public park in Texas founded by four freed slaves in 1872, where Muhammad Ali use to run when he was training in Houston (3018 Emancipation Avenue, www.emancipationparkconservancy.org).

74_ Parkwood Park

Walking in Queen Bey's footsteps

Parkwood Park isn't your average park. There's no playground, basketball court, or even a dog run. The setting is more pastoral, with rolling hills, a rarity among city parks, especially in Houston. The surrounding neighborhood, Riverside Terrace, is also an outlier – technically, part of the Third Ward, but with the quietness of the countryside. Standing apart as well is a former resident who ran laps in the park as a young girl. She now runs the world as an international music superstar, style slayer, designer, fierce feminist, social activist, philanthropist, wife, and mom to three children.

Of course, that would be Beyoncé, Miss Third Ward herself. Along with lyrical references and video shout-outs to her hometown, Beyoncé christened her athleisure line Ivy Park with a local acknowledgment. Her stylish sportswear brand combines her oldest daughter's middle name with the park down the street from her childhood home.

Glimpses of Parkwood Park appear in the brand's launch video, capturing the idyllic scenery, along with the official Parkwood Park sign in the Parks Department's green and white color scheme. That sign acts as a step and repeat for members of the Beyhive, often clad in Ivy Park attire, who get in formation against the backdrop of the young Beyoncé's old stomping grounds.

The pilgrimage continues with a view of the Knowles family home she shared with her younger sister and future one-name sensation, Solange. Little Beysearch is needed to find the location (3346 Parkwood Drive), as the two-story Colonial, built in 1935, is the only house on the block with a sign perched in the flower bed stating: *Private Residence*. Accordingly, bow down from a respectful distance. End at St. Mary's Montessori School (3006 Rosedale Street), where a seven-year-old Beyoncé won the talent show with a rendition of John Lennon's "Imagine." H-town vicious indeed.

Address 3400 North Parkwood Drive, Houston, TX 77021 | **Getting there** Bus 5, 54 to Scott Street & Parkwood Drive | **Hours** Daily dawn–dusk | **Tip** Beyoncé attended Houston's High School for the Performing and Visual Arts just long enough to have her freshman yearbook photo taken. Check out homegrown talent at the high school's new downtown campus, where performances, readings, and art shows are open to the public (790 Austin Street, www.houstonisd.org/hspva).

75 Peacock Records

You ain't nothing but a hound dog

The peacock is the showiest of the bird species. Confident and colorful, peacocks can also be aggressive when their turf is threatened. Don Robey, nightclub owner and music label maverick, undoubtedly would have selected the peacock as his spirit animal. As the founder of Peacock Records, based in the Fifth Ward neighborhood, Robey achieved a music history milestone as an African-American record label owner at a time when only white-owned major labels offered African-American artists an opportunity for chart-topping success. However, along with being a noteworthy promoter and producer, Robey was notorious as a man whose business dealings often included diamond rings on his fingers and a pistol by his side.

Robey's career in entertainment began with nightlife. Opening in 1946, his Bronze Peacock nightclub became the Fifth Ward's version of The Cotton Club in Harlem. Known for featuring the best in rhythm and blues, the club's music scene was a catalyst for the creation of Peacock Records in 1949. Robey operated from Lyons Avenue, the Fifth Ward's main drag, where he launched the career of Cajun bluesman Clarence "Gatemouth" Brown and staged the takeover of Memphis-based Duke Records.

Robey's righthand man was none other than Evelyn Johnson, a Black woman, who represented yet another breakthrough in the male-dominated music business. In 1953, Willie Mae "Big Mama" Thornton provided Peacock with one of its biggest hits, "Hound Dog," before the song was covered by Elvis Presley. As more songs landed on Billboard's Top 100, so did stories about Robey, whose recording empire ended in 1973.

A heart attack took Robey's life two years later. He left behind no tell-all memoir, but a historical marker, erected in 2011, attempts to set the record straight. Near the same Lyons Avenue address printed on Peacock's 45s, the legacy of the man before Motown lives on.

TEXAS HISTORICAL COMMISSION

TEXAS

PEACOCK RECORDS

DURING THE FIRST HALF OF THE 20TH CENTURY, THE MASS-MARKET RECORDINGS OF AFRICAN AMERICAN MUSICIANS WERE GROUPED UNDER THE TERM "RACE MUSIC," REGARDLESS OF THEIR MUSICAL GENRE, AND THESE MUSICIANS WERE MARKETED STRICTLY TO AFRICAN AMERICAN LISTENERS. IN 1949, A DECADE BEFORE THE BIRTH OF MOTOWN RECORDS, NIGHTCLUB OWNER DON D. ROBEY (1903-1975) SIGNED BLUES MUSICIAN CLARENCE "GATEMOUTH" BROWN TO A MANAGEMENT CONTRACT AND THEN DECIDED TO CREATE HIS OWN RECORD LABEL BECAUSE OF HIS DISSATISFACTION WITH THE TRADITIONAL "RACE MUSIC" MARKETING OFFERED BY THE MAJOR RECORD LABELS.

ROBEY'S PEACOCK RECORDS SOON OUTGREW AN OFFICE LOCATED AT 4104 LYONS, SO HE CONVERTED HIS FORMER DINNER CLUB, THE BRONZE PEACOCK AT 2809 ERASTUS, INTO A LARGER RECORDING STUDIO AND RELOCATED IN 1953. DURING THAT SAME YEAR, ROBEY ADDED DUKE RECORDS IN MEMPHIS, TENNESSEE TO HIS HOLDINGS AND CREATED BACK BEAT RECORDS AS A PEACOCK SUBSIDIARY. THE ACQUISITION OF DUKE RECORDS BROUGHT ROBEY THE CONTRACTS OF SEVERAL WELL-KNOWN ARTISTS, INCLUDING WILLIE MAE "BIG MAMA" THORNTON AND JOHNNY ACE. THE BELLS OF JOY AND THE FIVE BLIND BOYS OF MISSISSIPPI WERE AMONG MANY OF PEACOCK'S GOSPEL GROUPS.

MUCH OF THE SUCCESS OF DUKE-PEACOCK RECORDS CAN BE CREDITED TO THE SYSTEM OF UTILIZING NUMEROUS RECORDING STUDIOS, PRODUCTION PLANTS, AND DISTRIBUTORS AROUND THE COUNTRY TO REACH THE GREATEST NUMBER OF ARTISTS AND CUSTOMERS. THE RESULTING PROMINENCE WITHIN THE RECORD BUSINESS LED TO THE PURCHASE OF THE PEACOCK, DUKE, BACK BEAT AND SURE SHOT LABELS BY ABC-DUNHILL IN 1973, AND TODAY PEACOCK RECORDS IS REMEMBERED AS A PIONEERING MINORITY RECORDING FIRM.

MARKER IS PROPERTY OF THE STATE OF TEXAS   (2010)

Address 4120 Lyons Avenue, Houston, TX 77020 | Getting there Bus 11, 48 to Lyons Avenue & Featherstone Street | Hours Unrestricted | Tip Admire the DeLuxe Theater's sleek, streamline moderne exterior and check their calendar for a chance to go inside the recently renovated 1940s Fifth Ward movie house, where plays, lectures, and community events are held (3303 Lyons Avenue, www.thedeluxetheater.com).

76 Plant It Forward
Growing new roots

Since 2011, Plant It Forward has been securing parcels of land, like underutilized utility easements, around the city to help African refugees build their own urban farm businesses. Learning to transition their agricultural know-how from their homelands to Houston's year-round growing conditions, these skilled farmers produce a multitude of organic, non-GMO crops to be sold at area farmers markets and to supply top-rated restaurants.

Visitors are welcome at the four farm locations through a variety of events and programs. All are invited to pitch in during Community Work Days, where volunteers assist with tasks, like weeding and mulching. Urban Farm Experiences and special tours take you behind-the-scenes, while on-site pop-up farm stands are perfect for seeing where the flat of tomatoes you just purchased was grown. Locals meet the farmer growing their food when picking up their box of fruit and vegetables at the weekly farm share.

Challenging their customers' culinary skills, the refugee farmers incorporate crops from their home countries, like sugarcane, amaranth, and jute mallow leaves. In the summer, there will be bright red buds of rosella, or fresh hibiscus, more commonly found dried in the city's Hispanic markets for making *agua fresca*. In the fall, sweet potatoes come with their leaves in the farm's offerings, which are surprisingly easy to substitute for more familiar Southern greens.

Houston is proudly one of the most diverse cities in the United States, at one time accepting more refugees than any other city in the nation. In his Houston episode of *Parts Unknown*, the late Anthony Bourdain enjoyed a Congolese dinner party in the working garden. Several of the Plant It Forward farmers demonstrated how often it's through food that immigrants successfully assimilate to a new home – and enhance and influence local culture and cuisine.

Address 12581 Dunlap Street, Houston, TX 77035, +1 (713) 432-0754, www.plant-it-forward.org, info@plant-it-forward.org | Getting there Bus 47 to Dunlap Street & Fonmeadow Drive MB | Hours See website for farm stand hours, events, and tours | Tip Houston's only private farm inside the loop, Finca Tres Robles offers monthly farm tours and PIY (pick it yourself) Saturdays so you can learn more about their inventive agricultural operations (257 North Greenwood Street, www.fincatresrobles.org).

77 _ Post Oak Hotel Lobby
Making a sparkling entrance

The staff at the Post Oak Hotel gets fair warning when owner Tilman Fertitta arrives, given that his preferred parking spot is a helipad. As the star of reality TV show *Billion Dollar Buyer* and author of *Shut Up and Listen!*, Fertitta is no undercover boss. Consequently, there's nothing incognito about the Galveston-born billionaire, whose portfolio includes restaurants, casinos, the Houston Rockets, and the city's sole Five-Diamond AAA-rated hotel.

A transportation concierge assists guests who also wish to land on the hotel's private helipad, but most entrances are made through the lobby, where a substantial chunk of the $350 million building cost was spent. A sparkling, Swarovski crystal-laden, million dollar chandelier suspended overhead anchors the space. This light fixture most likely to inspire a fine jewelry line is a distant doppelganger for the five-ton chandelier dazzling patrons of the Dubai Opera House. Both chandelier installations share the same designer, Libor Sošťák, of the Czech lighting firm Lasvit, known for its contemporary take on Bohemian glassmaking techniques. The Post Oak's custom creation combines 1,428 LED lights and 738 crystal balls poised at the end of each wire like delicate droplets from the world's most lavish bubble bath.

However, there's artful competition taken from Fertitta's private collection. The lobby's MoMA envy inducing artwork features a trio of Frank Stella silkscreens with titles referencing *Moby Dick* on the right. A solo Stella sculptural piece jutting out of the wall hangs on the left.

After immersing yourself in the luxe surroundings, you might be tempted to make a grand entrance upon your return home. Shiny souvenirs can be found in the hotel's Rolls-Royce showroom, with a spiral staircase connecting two floors displaying the regal automobiles. Don't miss the swankiest auto repair shop waiting room in town.

Address 1600 West Loop South, Houston, TX 77027, +1 (346) 227-5000, www.thepostoakhotel.com | Getting there Bus 33 to Post Oak Boulevard & Hollyhurst Lane | Hours Unrestricted for hotel guests and visitors to the Post Oak's Spa and restaurants | Tip Make a VIP entrance at the Johnson Space Center with the Post Oak Hotel's Space Center Houston package that includes round-trip helicopter transportation, a local astronaut as your tour guide behind-the-scenes, and a starting price of $10,000.

78 Project Row Houses
Transformative art and preservation

Once lining the streets of Houston's oldest Black neighborhood, the shotgun-style row house is quickly becoming obsolete as developers fill the Third Ward with enclaves of modern townhomes. However, Project Row Houses provides visitors a glimpse of the past with a block of preserved row houses. In 1993, seven forward-thinking Black artists saved the 22 derelict structures as a place to showcase artwork and develop a community space to engage and revive the once-flourishing area through "social sculpture," a concept around art's potential to transform society.

With roots in West Africa, this architectural style first arrived in New Orleans in the early 1800s via Haitian immigrants and enslaved people before spreading along the Gulf Coast and becoming integral to the cultural landscape of many Southern cities, particularly in historically Black neighborhoods. Typically, these skinny, linear homes were one room wide and two to four rooms long. This straight shot floor plan created a natural, cooling air flow, an important pre-air conditioning amenity, while the close proximity of front porches created a social breezeway as a place for neighbors to gather, talk, and create tight-knit communities.

Project Row Houses and the restored structures now serve as one big porch for the Third Ward and Houston. Evolving over the years to meet the needs of the changing neighborhood and longtime residents, it's become harder to pin a label on this dynamic nonprofit. Art gallery, artist collective, community center, preservation society, small business incubator, and all-around change agent are just a few of the roles Project Row Houses plays.

But no matter whether you're stopping by to view the latest art exhibit, attend a meeting, or enjoy an evening performance, you'll always be welcomed by the bright white row of restored houses that started it all.

Address 2521 Holman Street, Houston, TX 77004, +1 (713) 526-7662,
www.projectrowhouses.org, info@projectrowhouses.org | **Getting there** Bus 9 to Holman
& Live Oak Street | **Hours** Unrestricted from outside; see website for events schedule |
Tip Stop in for a hug and a specialty double-stuffed cupcake from Ella Russell at her
Crumbville, TX bakery storefront, which came to fruition with the support of Project Row
Houses (2316 Elgin Street, www.crumbvilletx.com).

79__ The Rice Hotel

Jackie and JFK's last evening together

On November 21, 1963, President Kennedy sketched a small sail-boat on a piece of Rice Hotel letterhead – the last doodle of a pro-lific doodler. He and First Lady Jackie Kennedy spent a few hours of their final evening together in one of the hotel's suites before the couple addressed the League of United Latin American Citizens in the Crystal Ballroom. Later that night, they flew to Dallas, where he was assassinated the next day.

Fascinating anecdotes of famous guests and historical events fill the annals of the Rice Hotel and its downtown spot. Located on the corner of Texas Avenue and Main Street, the historic E-shaped building sits on the site of the Republic of Texas' capitol from 1837 to 1839. Successfully out-lobbying other cities for the honor, the Allen Brothers (see ch. 100 & 103) hurriedly built a two-story, wooden structure. However, Houston's muddy streets and mosquitoes had the politicians quickly retreating to Austin. The defunct government building operated as a hotel under various proprietors until it was razed in 1881. The successor, the five-story luxury Capitol Hotel, was snatched up by William Marsh Rice (see ch. 80) two years later, who renamed it the Rice Hotel.

In 1913, famous wheeler-dealer Jesse Jones rebuilt the Rice Hotel as the tallest building in the city, filling the 18 stories with luxuries, like a Turkish bath, a swimming pool, and a rooftop garden – a high society hotspot far above the dusty, noisy streets below. During the 1928 Democratic Convention, delegates partied on the rooftop in the evenings; some say you can still hear ghostly arguments. The hotel's grandeur attracted guests like Shirley Temple, the Eisen-howers, Neil Armstrong, and Mick Jagger, until fire code violations shut it down in 1977. Sitting empty for 20 years, it was reborn as private luxury apartments, where the lucky residents now call this historic address home.

Address 909 Texas Avenue, Houston, TX 77002 | Getting there METRORail to Preston (Red Line) | Hours Unrestricted from outside | Tip Book a stay at Houston's longest operating hotel, the Lancaster, which is still owned by the family of the original owner, Michele DeGeorge. Designed by famous local architect, Joseph Finger, the 12-story, 200-bedroom hotel was built in an impressive nine months, opening its doors on November 21, 1926 (701 Texas Avenue, www.thelancaster.com).

80 Rice Stadium
History on the field

After becoming 1949 Cotton Bowl Champions, the Rice University football team was rewarded with a brand-new stadium. Local contractor, Brown and Root, accomplished the legendary feat of building a 70,000-seat stadium in a mere eight months. Following a groundbreaking ceremony in February of 1950, crews worked nonstop to complete construction just in time for the Owls to win their season opener on September 30, 1950. Stadium seating is right on the field, giving this 70-year-old stadium bragging rights as one of the best places to watch a football game in the country, a high accolade in a state where the gridiron is as sacred as church.

The glory days of Rice football were short lived, but the stadium continued to host major events in Houston's history. Most famously, President John F. Kennedy gave his inspiring speech, "We choose to go to the moon," to a crowd of 40,000 gathered at the stadium on September 12, 1962. A plaque commemorating this historic moment just outside the stadium reads: *But why, some say, the moon? Why choose this as our goal? And they may well ask why climb the highest mountain? Why, 35 years ago, fly the Atlantic? Why does Rice play Texas?* –humorously referring to the school's current status as football underdogs.

However, the stadium was witness to more football history in 1974 when the Miami Dolphins defeated the Minnesota Vikings 24-7 in Super Bowl VIII. This game was the first time the Super Bowl was hosted in a venue without an NFL franchise. Only two other collegiate facilities still in use have hosted a Super Bowl. More recently, concerts have been the sellout events. Pink Floyd, The Eagles, Elton John, Billy Joel, and George Strait have taken to the field while Rice Owl fans wait for the football team's comeback.

While there will be better football days ahead, this is one stadium to visit for the history, not the pigskin – for now.

Address 6100 Main Street, Houston, TX 77005, +1 (713) 348-4077, www.riceowls.com |
Getting there Bus 27 to Greenbriar Drive & University Boulevard | Hours Exterior
unrestricted; see website for football schedule | Tip Instead of the usual retired jerseys and
championship banners that adorn university arenas, Rice's Tudor Fieldhouse's rafters are
festooned with banners boasting Nobel Laureates and Pulitzer Prize Winners (6100 Main
Street, www.riceowls.com/facilities/tudor-fieldhouse/4).

81 River Oaks Theatre

Last cinema standing

Megaplexes and moneyed real estate developers have made old-school movie houses an endangered species. The few remaining cinemas from the past now serve as event venues, like the Majestic Metro downtown and the Heights Theater, a lovingly restored live music haven. Others, like the Alabama Theatre, became a Trader Joe's, albeit a movie-themed one. But the marquee lights haven't dimmed at River Oaks Theatre.

Opening in 1939, this art deco cinema made its premiere along with the Alabama Theatre a short distance away. Ticket prices started out at 11 cents for a seat in the plush theater featuring ornate carvings depicting the land and sea on either side of the big screen. Many moviegoers came from the affluent River Oaks neighborhood and filled the 923 seats, including a balcony and a set of double wide "date night" seats.

The marquee became a cinema art house following the takeover by independent movie theater operator Landmark Theatres in 1976. For the next decade, foreign films and cult classics dominated the screening calendar – cherished by regulars who included Texas director Richard Linklater. Countless Houstonians became movie buffs watching films ranging from raunchy *Pink Flamingos* to the innovative Talking Heads concert film, *Stop Making Sense*. As movie screens multiplied, the River Oaks followed suit by carving out two smaller theaters from the balcony, along with a bar.

The marquee got the star treatment hosting a local premiere for *RoboCop 2*, starring Peter Weller, who brought his mom to see the movie where downtown Houston stood in for a dire Detroit.

In 2007, the theater received protected landmark status, but demolition still threatens. But until then, the roster of indie films and midnight movies, including a monthly live screening of *The Rocky Horror Picture Show*, keeps this cinematic shrine a neighborhood movie house for the entire city.

Address 2009 West Gray Street, Houston, TX 77019, +1 (713) 524-2175,
www.landmarktheatres.com/houston/river-oaks-theatre | Getting there Bus 32 to
West Gray & McDuffie Street | Hours See website for showtimes | Tip In November,
the Houston Cinema Arts Society holds a multi-venue film festival with panels
and special guests, including past participants Tilda Swinton and Isabella Rossellini
(www.cinemahtx.org).

82 Rockefeller's

Double trouble

"If you're over 40, you remember the concerts; if you're under 40, you remember the weddings," says Rockefeller's booking manager Mike Sims. He is familiar with the venue's shifts from music club, to banquet hall, to its present incarnation hosting receptions and bands. Even the building's bank origins include two name changes, both still visible on this neoclassical structure built in 1925. Rockefeller's multifaceted history is exemplified by both a listing on the National Register of Historic Places and their roster of musicians whose names are now part of the Rock and Roll Hall of Fame.

Corinthian columns and ornamental cherubs trimmed with mermaid tails made a statement on this commercial corner near the Heights, one of the city's first suburbs. The building was destined for greatness, given the grand design by Joseph Finger, an Austrian immigrant-turned-architect in high demand. First opening as Citizen State Bank in 1925, this bank's initials remain on a medallion at the entrance.

In 1946, the building re-emerged as Heights State Bank, along with rumors that Bonnie and Clyde had robbed it. Tall tales about the Barrow Gang persist too, easily conjured up by a weathered night depository door left ajar outside.

After the bank's closure and a period as office space, the building became Rockefeller's in 1979, a music club named for its high finance past. Concertgoers stood where customers once waited for a teller in front of a stage bearing the bank's motto overhead. Bands congregated in the vault-turned-dressing room with a rebar-reinforced concrete entry signaling high security. The club's flyers reflected the city's live music heyday with the pride and joy of performances belonging to native Texan, guitar master, Stevie Ray Vaughan. Rockefeller's ownership changed hands, but the experience remains the same for wedding guests and music fans.

Address 3620 Washington Avenue, Houston, TX 77007, +1 (713) 862-4070, www.rockefellershouston.com | Getting there Bus 85 to Washington Avenue & Heights Boulevard | Hours Unrestricted from the outside; see website for event calendar | Tip View Joseph Finger's art deco modernist design at Houston's City Hall, which was built in 1939 (901 Bagby Street, www.houstontx.gov).

83 Roop Sari Palace
Marriage material

With approximately 150,000 Indian-Americans living in Houston, it's only a matter of time before you're invited to a Desi wedding, with multiple celebrations lasting up to a week and requiring as many costume changes as a Bollywood blockbuster. Whether you're a guest, bride, or groom, the next stop will likely be the Mahatma Gandhi District, designated in 2010 in recognition of the South Asian community's cultural and commercial presence in the area.

However, many of the businesses along Hillcroft Avenue and Harwin Drive have been long-standing fixtures on these streets crowded with *chaat* shops, tucked away Hindu temples, and 22k gold jewelers. Roop Sari Palace, a family-run boutique, has been outfitting other people's families for over 25 years. Many of the saleswomen, affectionately called "aunties" by brides-to-be, have been on the bridal suite floor for almost as long.

Customers travel from nearby cities and states to shop the collection featuring the latest looks imported from India. In true Houston melting pot fashion the staff speaks multiple languages, including Spanish because many young women have chosen the spectacularly embellished ensembles for their *quinceañera* attire. Sari-wearing newbies get an assist from the team of tailors, who insert hooks throughout the seven yards of fabric to prevent a wardrobe malfunction.

When it comes to jewelry, artfully organized by color, the only difficulty is deciding. Bangles, traditionally worn by the bride and often purchased in bulk as party favors, beckon from a floor-to-ceiling display. *Jhumka* earrings, named for their umbrella-like shape, gently jingle as customers examine their intricate designs. The younger generation now favors faux gems over heirloom finery, allowing for more and bigger bling. But no matter what's trending in wedding wear, *roop*, meaning beauty, is always in style.

Address 6655 Harwin Drive, Suite 101-B, Houston, TX 77036, +1 (713) 278-7667, www.roopsaripalace.com, roopsaripalace@gmail.com | Getting there Bus 47 to Hillcroft Street & Harwin Drive | Hours Mon & Wed–Sat 11am–8pm, Sun noon–8pm | Tip Design isn't an afterthought at Raja Sweets, where Indian confections fill elegant gift boxes at this bakery, which has been a mainstay of the area since 1986 (5667 Hillcroft Avenue, www.rajahouston.com).

84 Rosario's Mistic Yerberia

Step into a healing arts dispensary

The positive energy vortex of Rosario's Mistic Yerberia starts as soon as you pull into the parking lot. Large posters of the shop's owner Maria Rosario Angle on her recent spiritual vacation to Machu Picchu and winning nights at the casino adorn the property's fence. Customers are greeted by the bright, cheery, yellow storefront and sidewalk decorated with pictures of guardian angels, saints, and symbols of good fortune. Portraits of Maria's two mystical mentors, her grandmother and father, guard the shop's entrance.

Maria began learning the powers of herbs, blessings, and cleansings at the age of five while wrapping purchases in her grandmother's *yerberia* in Nuevo Laredo, Mexico. Now, she has been serving the East End community, a neighborhood with strong Hispanic roots, for over 35 years with her own expertise in botanicals and highly-attuned powers of divination.

Book a personal session with this third-generation healer who uses her intuition and combined knowledge of the tarot, Santeria, and Catholic faith to connect with her clients and guide them through their life questions and personal troubles. After an insightful reading in her office, Maria performs any needed rituals at her small altar in the adjacent room. Her services aren't limited to people either. Her cleansing of a continually broken-down art car led to its first-prize win in the annual Art Car Parade (see ch. 6).

For a DIY solution, the store is stocked with candles, incense, statuary, crystals, amulets, and spiritual oils for every petition or problem. Need things to go your way in the courtroom? Wear a splash of *Caso de Corte* perfume. Headed to the casinos? Burn the *Los 3 Budas* candle. Want to work on releasing your negative emotions and blockages? Add your name to the list for Maria's special monthly, full moon foot soak blend. Whatever your need, Maria and her *yerberia* have the answer.

Address 5306 Canal Street, Houston, TX 77011, +1 (832) 968-7233, www.rosariosmisticshoponline.com | **Getting there** Bus 20 to Canal & North Delmar Street | **Hours** Mon–Fri 10am–6pm, Sat 10am–5pm | **Tip** Houston's foremost pagan religious supplier, Magick Cauldron, has been peddling wands, chalices, and its popular Port-a-Witch kit for over 26 years. Tarot card readings and spellcasting consultations are available from the supernatural experts on staff (2424 Montrose Boulevard, www.magickcauldron.com).

85 Saint Martin's Kneelers
Heavenly threads

The tony Tanglewood neighborhood filled with Texas Tuscan mansions suddenly turns medieval on the corner of Woodway Drive and Sage Road. A gothic cathedral – seemingly transported from the Middle Ages, with spires stretching 188 feet above the street – is home to the largest Episcopalian congregation in the United States. Completed in 2004, St. Martin's Church took divine design inspiration from St. Elisabeth's Church in Marburg, Germany, built in 1235. Even the church bells have an impressive lineage, having been cast by the same foundry as Big Ben and the Liberty Bell.

The 9,000-member congregation also had a hands-on role in the creation of this sacred space: 750 parishioners paraded 4,555 organ pipes into the sanctuary for the installation of the church's custom-made Gloria Dei organ. Ordinary objects are also made extraordinary in this house of worship. A network of needle-pointers, known as the St. Martin Saintly Stitchers, transforms the cushioned kneelers along the communion rail and in the pews into works of spiritual art. The group began their ongoing efforts with the altar rail before taking on the kneelers in the church's 300 pews, hand-stitching Scripture verses to match the adjacent stained-glass windows depicting scenes from the Bible.

Some of those stitches were made by former First Lady and church member Barbara Bush, who displayed a "needlework tree" created by her fellow stitchers at the White House in 1991. She also mentioned her handiwork on two kneelers and an appreciation for the craft circle's camaraderie in an unfinished letter to her children shortly before she died. In a fitting tribute, the stitching collective's cranberry red kneeler cushions were used by past presidents and political VIPs at Mrs. Bush's 2018 memorial service, which was followed seven months later by another gathering to honor her husband, President George H. W. Bush.

Address 717 Sage Road, Houston, TX 77056, +1 (713) 621-3040, www.stmartinsepiscopal.org |
Getting there Bus 47 to Woodway Drive & Sage Road | Hours See website for services and
docent-led tour schedules | Tip Pamper your soles at Tanglewood Nails, a friendly salon just
a few blocks away from the church where the Bushes were regulars (5750 Woodway Drive,
Suite 132, www.tanglewoodnailspa.com).

86 Sam Houston Boat Tour

Cruise Houston's waterborne highway

A port city that no one thinks of as a port city, Houston lacks the maritime lore of its Gulf Coast cousin, New Orleans. But the port makes up for it in size as the largest container port in the region and first in the United States in foreign waterborne tonnage. Since 1928, the Houston Port Authority has been providing free boat tours of the ship channel to help educate the public about the vital role the port and its operations play in Houston's and the world's economies.

Tugboats, barges, cranes, grain elevators, and wharves provide the backdrop for this overlooked waterway cruise of the Houston Ship Channel via the M/V *Sam Houston II*. Since the vessel's christening in 1958, over two million passengers have made the 90-minute round trip voyage featuring a narrated tour and panoramas of international cargo vessels, some stacked high with containers holding everything from rhinos to uranium, and others with James Bond-style yachts and pleasure crafts hoisted on lifting belts.

Houston's "Petro Metro" nickname comes to life with a landscape of refineries as the boat turns around at the Turning Basin Terminal, just 52 miles from the Gulf of Mexico. Nearby is the location where General Santa Anna was captured after his defeat by Sam Houston, the vessel's namesake, in the 1836 Battle of San Jacinto delivering Texas its independence from Mexico (see ch. 87).

This tour offers the only opportunity for an up-close view of the United States' second largest port, so celebrities, politicians, and dignitaries regularly include the tour on their Houston itinerary, even royal siblings, Princess Anne and Prince Charles. If you're not a VIP, be sure to allow plenty of time before your scheduled departure, as trains commonly block the gate entrance. If you happen to get blocked, think of trainspotting as a bonus glimpse of the inner workings of one of the busiest ports in the world.

Address 7300 Clinton Drive, Houston, TX 77020, +1 (713) 670-2631, www.porthouston.com/sam-houston-boat-tour | Getting there Interstate 610 East Loop to exit 28 Clinton Drive continue west on Clinton Drive to Gate 8 | Hours See website for tour schedule, reservation required | Tip Stroll along Navigation Esplanade in the Second Ward, where Gary Sweeney's massive faux-wood anchor sculpture is a nod to the neighborhood's historical ties to the port (2800 Navigation Boulevard).

87 San Jacinto Battleground

Where we remember the Alamo

With over two million tourists trekking to the Alamo every year, there's little chance anyone will forget the site of the siege in San Antonio. And yet the victorious finale of Texas Independence, an 18-minute assault of vengeance and valor – and the battle where soldiers first cried, "Remember the Alamo!" – seems to get second billing.

The San Jacinto Battleground, located approximately 20 miles from downtown Houston, looks much the same as it did in 1836, absent the opposing forces, of course. The park's 1,200 acres encourage history buffs to envision their own documentary against the backdrop of trees that once shielded Texas troops from the enemy's view. Buffalo Bayou and the San Jacinto River still meet in the same spot Sam Houston selected to launch the attack against Santa Anna and his posse of 6,000 soldiers. Shortly before sunset, the wide open space takes on an amber hue, allowing visitors to bask in the historic glory of the site (see ch. 86).

But there's more than memories here. The San Jacinto Monument is the park's centerpiece. A 220-pound star, with five points visible to admirers from every angle, crowns the top of the stately column, rising 567.31 feet, or 12.31 feet taller than the Washington Monument. Inside, a museum of Texas history and treasures provides a link to the past. Some objects are sentimental, like Sam Houston's gold ring, gifted by his mother when he joined the Army and inscribed with the word *Honor*, which never left the Texas Revolution hero's finger. Others represent the spoils of war, like Santa Anna's flashy knee buckle with four missing gemstones seized and awarded as victory spoils.

Take the 36-second elevator ride with an attendant – and often half a dozen school kids – to the top of the tower, where views of the Houston Ship Channel await. Visit this historic site and remember the Alamo, but also remember San Jacinto.

Address One Monument Circle, La Porte, TX 77571, +1 (281) 479-2421, www.sanjacinto-museum.org | **Getting there** By car, take Highway 225 east to La Porte and exit Independence Parkway, turn left and continue through the park gates | **Hours** Daily 9am–6pm | **Tip** See the site where Santa Anna was captured and the makings of the "Yellow Rose of Texas" legend about the lady who pulled a Mata Hari on the Mexican general. From Highway 225, take Shaver Street north. Turn on the Pasadena Paper Mill entrance road at Washburn Tunnel. Turn right at the old plant gate. The marker is on the right about 100 feet ahead.

88__Screwed Up Records and Tapes

Diary of the Originator

Contrary to its name, customers won't find records or tapes at this storefront that's considered the equivalent of a UNESCO site for Southern hip-hop. It's actually named for the late DJ Screw's chopped up, slowed down sound. Originally recorded on cassettes, DJ Screw's tracks coated with his hazy sonic veneer are sold on CDs only, cataloged in binders and labeled as chapters, like a book of hip-hop psalms. Therefore, driving to the shop is advised, preferably in a car still equipped with a CD player for immediate aural gratification.

Fans snap selfies with murals celebrating the musician whose once-underground sound is now the subject of a museum exhibition. Even the shop's exterior was used as the backdrop for Houston rapper Travis Scott's *Sicko Mode* video, filmed with Drake, who namechecks DJ Screw in his songs. Owners of slabs, custom cars with shiny paint jobs, often stage photo shoots in the parking lot too.

But what if you're new to DJ Screw's slowed and throwed remixes? Begin with a phone call to the shop for a one-minute freestyle recording of the hours and location by Houston rapper and Screwed Up Click (SUC) member E.S.G. Next, bring cash for your transaction, which will be made through a plexiglass window in homage to DJ Screw's DIY sales of his "gray tapes" from his home.

While the whiteboard listing the CDs can be overwhelming, DJ Screw's family and friends who run the shop advise Screwhead beginners to start with *Chapter 12*, featuring the SUC in a 35-minute shout-out jam session called "June 27th." If you're thirsty, a hip-hop-themed Exotic Pop vending machine (see ch. 30) offers sodas named for local rappers. No doubt you'll leave with the sentiment, *Wish Screw Were Here*, printed on a T-shirt (available for purchase).

Address 3538 West Fuqua Street, Houston, TX 77045, +1 (713) 434-2888, www.screweduprecords.com | Getting there By car, take Highway 288 South to the Almeda Genoa exit. Turn right and continue onto West Fuqua Street. | Hours Daily 2–9pm | Tip The Houston Hip Hop Research Collection, overseen by University of Houston archivist Julie Grob, showcases the founders of Htown's signature sound, including DJ Screw, Geto Boys, Slim Thug, Pimp C, and Bun B (UH Libraries Special Collections, 4333 University Drive, libraries.uh.edu/locations/special-collections/houston-hip-hop).

89__Serenity Knives

Blade runners

A week before Thanksgiving, one of the busiest businesses in the city isn't a grocery store, bakery, liquor shop, or a therapist's office. Rather, it's a small workshop on a quiet block lined with quaint bungalows in the Heights neighborhood. For those with turkey duty, the blade-smiths of Serenity Knives are sharpening saviors whose Japanese water stones and grinding belts turn out razor-sharp cutlery for the most important family feast of the year.

For the rest of the year, the shop resembles a microcosm of occupations reflected in the tools brought in for rehab, from surgical instruments to a slicer used to make pickled pig skins. But most notably, owner Russell Montgomery and his crew of artisans create custom knives for all occasions.

Montgomery's handiwork made headlines when a custom set of 22 steak knives appeared in diners' hands at Oxheart, helmed by chef Justin Yu, who would later win the James Beard award for Best Chef in the Southwest before closing the restaurant in 2017. Fine dining chefs followed suit, commissioning Montgomery to create knives, including one with a handle fashioned from *oosik*, a fossilized penis bone formerly belonging to a walrus.

While unusual materials like giraffe bone, which takes color well due to its density, are attention-getting, Montgomery's artistry is what makes him a magnet for knife collectors. Whether the client desires a hunting knife, a champagne saber, or a replica of the Beastmaster sword, the final product is informed by a blend of knife-making traditions. Montgomery's respect for both the perfection-driven precision of the Japanese craft he learned under Murray Carter, a 17th-generation Yoshimoto bladesmith, as well as the rugged practicality of Appalachia, translates into the functional elegance on display in the shop's showroom. In turn, customers ensure the time-honored craft of knife-making never dulls.

Address 410 Harvard Street, Houston, TX 77007, +1 (832) 860-4754, www.serenityknives.com, russell@serenityknives.com | **Getting there** Bus 40, 66 to Heights Boulevard & Fourth Street | **Hours** Tue–Sat 10am–6pm | **Tip** Carry on the tradition of board and video games at Coral Sword, a gamer's hangout and coffee shop named for the prized weapon in the Final Fantasy series (1318 Telephone Road, Suite 3, www.coralsword.com).

90 S.H.A.P.E. Community Center

Cooking up collective good

The best-kept food secret in the city is inside a cheery, mural-covered building in the Third Ward. The café at S.H.A.P.E. Community Center is taken over daily by different chefs kickstarting their entrepreneurial dreams and honing their culinary skills, all for the center's benefit. The open-air commercial kitchen is a cross between a breakfast diner counter and a chef's tasting table, where you're likely to strike up a conversation with the staff as they prepare your meal. Depending on the day, you can sample Southern comfort food, Creole/Caribbean fusion, or even vegan alkaline-friendly smoothies and herbal teas.

An acronym for Self-Help for African People through Education, S.H.A.P.E. Community Center started as a small youth initiative to help area kids walk to school safely, and it blossomed into the heart of the Third Ward, where the community continues to gather to help. Founded in 1969, the center quickly filled the need for a non-religious, non-political space where the whole gamut of the Civil Rights Movement was welcome to meet and work together to fight racial injustice. It earned the nickname, the "United Nations of the Hood."

The secret to S.H.A.P.E.'s continued success is the people who support and run the place. Deloyd Parker, Jr., a longtime community and civil rights activist, has been the executive director from day one, creating an atmosphere where the staff is deeply committed to changing lives, and where volunteers build deep-rooted connections to the center's work, often donating their time and talents for decades. There's always a buzz in the building, whether it's from the energetic young people attending after-school programs, or the seniors who serve on the Elders Institute of Wisdom, guardians of the community's culture and fountains of knowledge. And S.H.A.P.E.'s café is the best place to meet all these remarkable people in person.

Address 3815 Live Oak Street, Houston, TX 77004, +1 (713) 521-0641, www.shape.org, shape@shape.org | Getting there Bus 09 to Holman & Live Oak Street | Hours See website for café hours | Tip After a structural roof leak during Hurricane Harvey caused major damage to the historically registered Blue Triangle Community Center building, the organization raised funds for the monumental restoration project. For a small donation, you can view their progress and learn more of Blue Triangle's history of empowering women of color since 1919 (3005 McGowen Street, www.the-bluetriangle.org).

91 __ Shoeshine Charley's Big Top Lounge

Three drink circus

Step into the red glow of Shoeshine Charley's Big Top Lounge, where live music competes for attention with walls decked out in old Ringling Brothers and Barnum & Bailey advertisements, unnerving clown art, antique beer signs, Elvis memorabilia, and a heist-worthy Pink Panther painting on black velvet. Guarding the loft space above the front door are a trio of musical rats who once played on an Astroworld carnival ride. A hidden switch controls the accompanying acrobat clown, who maniacally flips over his high bar on slow repeat when activated.

It's an unlikely sports bar, but owner Pete Gordon is a team fanatic. If the Astros are playing, the baseball game will be on the two small, square TVs behind the bar. His Polish Pete & the Polka? I Hardly Know Her Band recorded the viral hit, "The Altuve Polka," amid the 2017 World Series mania, landing them the honor of leading the World Series Championship victory parade.

Bordering the bar's ceiling are vintage circus paintings from the toy store that occupied the space in the 1940s and 1950s. A character resembling Geoffrey the Giraffe is rumored to be the prototype for the Toys "R" Us logo. These funhouse murals inspired the "Big Top" part of the bar's name when they were discovered above the drop ceiling that had been protecting them from past, bland office renovations.

The lounge also bears the name of the late master of ceremonies at the Continental Club, the sister music club next door. "Shoeshine" Charley Miller was notorious for his colorful band introductions – the more he liked an artist, the more he butchered their name. Placed prominently beside the tiny stage, Miller's shoeshine stand still watches over the small bar, where his ghost is likely cursing all the sneaker-wearing customers.

Address 3714 Main Street, Houston, TX 77002, +1 (713) 529-9899, www.continentalclub.com/bigtop | Getting there METRORail to Ensemble/HCC (Red Line) | Hours Tue 7pm–midnight, Wed & Thu 9pm–1:30am, Fri–Sun 8pm–2am | Tip The nearby tiki-loving record store Sig's Lagoon decorates their walls from floor to ceiling with Texas music clippings (3622 Main Street, Suite E, www.sigslagoon.com).

92 Silos at Sawyer Yards

The sweet smell of success

Houston's status as the world's energy capital overshadows its agrarian past. Galleria mall goers shop unaware of the rural flatland that's now Neiman Marcus. The annual Houston Rodeo's Livestock Show is the only exposure most city slickers get to farm life. However, there's evidence of Houston's agricultural prowess reinvented for the urban dweller.

In the 1900s, Texas rice production ramped up with an assist from Seito Saibara, a Japanese farmer invited by the Chamber of Commerce to share his rice-growing expertise. Shonpei Mykwaya, a Japanese immigrant who introduced rice farming to the Gulf Coast town of Santa Fe, was even honored with a road bearing his surname. Houston acted as the commodity's command center, and the 1960s ushered in Riviana Foods' colossal concrete rice silos branded with logos of fan favorites, Success and Mahatma Rice.

Riviana's rice processing empire wasn't in the boonies. Instead, its First Ward location was minutes from downtown, and the plant's proximity to the Union Pacific railroad made for optimized operations. But like the oil bust in the 1880s, rice growing in Texas took a downturn. The decline continued with less land dedicated to the diminishing cash crop every year. In 2008, Riviana left Houston for Memphis, building a facility closer to the Arkansas farmers who made rice their state's top agricultural export.

Now, galleries have replaced the rice once stored in the 34 silos. Part of an industrial complex turned creative campus, the Silos at Sawyer Yards join the area's vast art studio acreage. SITE Gallery Houston, still sporting the Riviana rice brand signage, hosts site-specific installations created by artists facing the atypical constraint of a gallery with a grain hopper overhead. While exhibitions are temporary, the silos are a permanent fixture, confirmation that ingenuity and industry are a recipe for success.

Address 1502 Sawyer Street, Houston, TX 77007, www.sawyeryards.com | **Getting there** Bus 30 to Sawyer Street & Washington Avenue | **Hours** See website for events | **Tip** 800 feet of murals await onlookers in Art Alley, located in the shadow of the Silos on the Sawyer Yards campus. On the second Saturday of each month, Art Alley is home to a pop-up market, and neighboring art studios open their doors to the public (1502 Sawyer Street, www.fresharts.org/top-attractions/art-alley-at-sawyer-yards).

93 Silver Slipper

One more Saturday night

Both first-timers and loyal patrons can expect a handshake and a hug during a musical sojourn at the Silver Slipper, one of the city's last rhythm and blues clubs with a well-loved patina that's both refined and relaxed. Curley Cormier, the club's owner, is the one with the firm but gentle grip, which he also uses on guitar and deejaying between sets with the house band. Warm embraces come from Curley's wife Dorothy, positioned behind the bar. Her spunky niece Veronica is the "five-dollar lady," who collects the cover charge at the door. Cherry, a two-year club veteran, balances trays of beers and buckets of ice to tables, usually all full by 10pm.

A family affair from the start, the Silver Slipper has good genes. Curley's father first transformed the former ice cream parlor into a zydeco hotspot where Clifton Chenier, later heralded as the king of the genre, played. Curley's sister briefly owned the club long enough to christen it the Silver Slipper before the couple took over in 1973.

One secret to success, according to Dorothy, is keeping the place just the way regulars have liked it for years: tidy tables, lights kept low with a red glow, and a menu of fried catfish, pork chops, and wings. Waitresses deliver set-ups to customers, who bring their own libations, like Betty Boo, who holds court at her designated table when she's not shimmying on the checkerboard dance floor.

As the band warms up, the audience readies themselves for two sets of soul and swagger. Guest vocalists command the mike between instrumental jams. Getting in the groove, Curley dips his guitar low, and keyboardist Mike Stone stands up. A line dance forms, while couples sway on the side. For birthdays, the band serenades the honoree with a wish for many more. It's a wish shared by all who gather here on a Saturday night – that there will be many more such nights at the Silver Slipper.

Address 3717 Crane Street, Houston, TX 77026, +1 (713) 673-9004 | Getting there Bus 003 to Wipprecht & Crane Street | Hours Live music Sat only 8pm–2am | Tip Look for the historical marker along Eastex Freeway and Collingsworth Street dedicated to the Creole residents of Frenchtown, who contributed zydeco to the city's soundtrack. *Laissez les bons temps rouler* at the Big Easy on Sunday nights with live zydeco music (5731 Kirby Drive, www.thebigeasyblues.com).

94 Sound Figure

Do you hear what I hear?

Don't look for *Sound Figure* at the Menil Collection or seek an explanatory placard. Instead, use your ears to find this elusive aural field approximately 20 feet from the main entrance doors. This sound installation goes unnoticed by most visitors who don't realize that the almost imperceptible, chime-like noise is actually a work of art commissioned by the Menil in 2006. Created by the late musician/artist Max Neuhaus, who also stashed sound art under a Times Square traffic island, *Sound Figure* is a fine reward for highly attuned visitors and in-the-know art lovers. The auditory object of art does present a technical challenge to the conservation team who wrestle with the piece's intermittent output.

Even unplugged, *Sound Figure* represents the museum's approach to engaging all the senses. Since 1987, the Menil Collection, founded by art-collecting activist Dominique de Menil, encourages a free-range approach to viewing art without the typical museum offerings of audio tours and apps. The Menil Collection's unconventional location in the leafy Montrose neighborhood – and its free entry – also sets this 30,000-square-foot art space apart from big-city, blue-chip art museums. Encompassing 30 acres, the Menil grounds cater to locals who often spend more time on the grassy lawns than the galleries displaying Rothkos, Byzantine icons, and instruments from the Pacific Islands.

However, there's nothing static about the interior. The element of surprise informs the museum's approach to art installation. Your favorite Magritte will move without announcement. But rest assured that another masterpiece will replace it. Like *Sound Figure*, the museum contains artful hidden treasures – a tiny, hand-carved mask tucked away in an alcove or indigenous artifacts suspended from the ceiling. The sun's rays magically filter through the Renzo Piano-designed building bringing a sense of enlightenment to every visit.

Address 1533 Sul Ross Street, Houston, TX 77006, +1 (713) 525-9400, www.menil.org, info@menil.org | Getting there Bus 25 to Richmond Avenue & Loretto Drive | Hours Wed–Sun 11am–7pm | Tip Look down for the weathered steel sculptures created by land art pioneer Michael Heizer, whose works are embedded in the Menil Collection's front lawn and next to the Menil Drawing Institute.

95 Space Shuttle Gantry
Walk in the footsteps of astronauts

Greeting tourists from all over the world to NASA's Johnson Space Center is Independence Plaza, the museum's newest addition dedicated to the retired Space Shuttle Program. The colossal centerpiece is *Independence*, a life-sized shuttle replica, piggybacked on a NASA 905, one of only two Shuttle Carrier Aircraft (SCA) used to ferry shuttles around the country. The two aircraft are the basis for an eight-story, 5,500-square-foot building. Inside this engineering feat, explore the flight deck and the astronauts' close living quarters on the model shuttle before continuing below to the modified fuselage showcasing historical footage, fun facts, and interactive exhibits where you can conduct your own stress tests.

However, one of the most remarkable artifacts is actually behind the NASA 905. Follow in the footsteps of the hundreds of astronauts who used the orbiter access arm from Kennedy Space Center's launch pad 39B to board the shuttle before leaving Earth. From 1986 to 2006, this original gantry, 147 feet above the ground, spanned the gap between the launch tower and the entry hatch for 53 shuttle missions. Decommissioned and removed in 2009, the walkway and its clean environment entry space, called the "white room," eventually made its 1,000+ mile journey along the interstates from Florida to Houston as an extra-wide load.

If walking the path of former astronauts inspires the space geek in you, you can take the experience one step further and sign up for Space Center University. During these five-day programs, go behind the scenes of the astronauts' training and work facilities, where you can experience zero gravity on Earth in the Neutral Buoyancy Lab and learn how to build a robotic rover to accomplish tasks on Mars. You can also fuel your curiosity by attending the free (with a reservation) monthly Thought Leaders Lectures series with experts on the future of space exploration.

Address 1601 NASA Road 1, Houston, TX 77058, +1 (281) 244-2100, www.spacecenter.org, schinfo@spacecenter.org | **Getting there** By car, I-45 south to exit 24 toward NASA 1, follow signs | **Hours** Mon–Fri 10am–7pm, Sat & Sun 9am–7pm | **Tip** You can often see longhorns grazing in the adjacent pastures while riding the NASA tram and exploring Rocket Park. This trophy steer herd belongs to The Longhorn Project at Johnson Space Center, a hands-on educational program offering school tours of their working ranch and gardens (www.thelonghornproject.com).

96 __ Spanish Village

Try your luck at Lotería

Spanish Village has been serving Houstonians tequila-heavy margaritas and cheese enchiladas smothered in chili gravy since 1953, earning bragging rights as one of the oldest Tex-Mex restaurants in the city. The Pico brothers, Larry and Alfonso, started the restaurant in a small brick house that was built in the 1880s on Almeda Road. Today, servers use the home's front porch steps to carry trays of smoking hot plates from the kitchen, which is through the original front door marked by the still-present mailbox slot.

Despite the restaurant's telenovela-worthy family feuds, including one trademark spat that left the restaurant briefly renamed Larry Pico's Village in the 1990s, and its hodge-podge architecture that includes a few patio enclosures and moving entrance, much of Spanish Village has stayed remarkably unchanged. The mosaic-tiled tables from 1955 are still cemented to the floor. The chef still prepares Alfonso's original recipes written in a yellowed, dog-eared notebook. And the ceiling is still strung with multicolored Christmas lights, maracas, and *papel picado*.

What has changed is that the Pico family is now in an advisory role. A youthful Abhi Sreerama assumed ownership in 2018 with every intention of preserving the restaurant's history while spicing it up with a few new traditions. His most popular additions include adding his wife's decadent *tres leches* cake on the menu and a *Lotería* night on the first Wednesday of every month. For this Mexican version of bingo, staff pass out *tablas* and bowls of dried black beans to mark off the images that are used instead of numbers. One patron shuffles the deck for Abhi, who then calls out the cards in Spanish until the lucky winner yells, "*¡Lotería!*" The sombrero-wearing victor's photo is added to the thousands of celebratory Polaroids that have covered the walls of this Tex-Mex institution for decades.

Address 4720 Almeda Road, Houston, TX 77004, +1 (713) 523-2861, www.spanishvillagetx.com, hi@spanishvillagerestaurant.com | **Getting there** Bus 11 to Almeda Road & Blodgett Street | **Hours** Tue–Sat 11am–9pm, Sun 10am–2pm | **Tip** Get your daubers ready for a spirited evening of "Not Your Granny's Bingo" at SPJST Lodge 88. Every Thursday, crowds pack the hall, celebrating birthdays and divorces while keeping up with the fast-paced caller (1435 Beall Street, www.lodge88.org/bingo).

97__Spirit of the Bayou
Born on the bayou

With over 2,500 miles of waterways making up Houston's numerous bayous, it's no wonder "Bayou City" was one of its earliest nicknames. Disembark on a nautical journey through the city aboard the Buffalo Bayou Partnership's pontoon boat, *Spirit of the Bayou*. Since 2005, the guardians of this grand outdoor resource have welcomed visitors aboard their tours to gain a new perspective of the city's skyline and appreciation of the slow-moving, murky waters teeming with wildlife and history.

Anyone who thinks Houston has lost all its past to wrecking balls hasn't seen the many layers of history that are prevalent along the banks of Buffalo Bayou. Guided by locals, the historical boat tours narrate the forgotten tales of an early Houston, inviting you to imagine a bustling Allen's Landing, Houston's birthplace and first port, where large ships docked to unload their cargo for waiting merchants. Guides point out incredible landmarks hidden by development, like the railway suspension bridge designed by Joseph Strauss, the architectural engineer of the Golden Gate Bridge.

The "Port to Port" tour journeys east of Downtown towards the Gulf of Mexico, where the bayou widens and the tidal waters that can flow in either direction become brackish, making it possible to spot blue crabs below the surface and pelicans taking flight. Even on the short 30-minute excursion, you're likely to see herons, eagles, snapping turtles, fish, nutria, and the odd alligator.

Set sail at sunset for a special view of the Waugh Bridge bat colony's nightly emergence, when the state's second-largest colony of Mexican free-tailed bats eats three tons of insects each night – hopefully, all mosquitos, Houstonians number one predator. While the themed seasonal tours sell out quickly, you can always chart your own adventure for a private viewing of the bayou's rich history and lush scenery.

Address 1005 Commerce Street, Houston, TX 77002, +1 (713) 752-0314, www.buffalobayou.org/boat-tours, info@buffalobayou.org | **Getting there** Bus 20 to Franklin & Main Street | **Hours** See website for schedule | **Tip** Reserve a tour of the Buffalo Bayou Park Cistern, a decommissioned underground water reservoir built in 1926 that's often the site of temporary art installations and special sessions for amateur photographers (105 Sabine Street, buffalobayou.org/visit/destination/the-cistern).

98 St. Arnold Brewing Company

Beers and icons

When the oldest craft brewery in Texas built a new restaurant in 2018, it created a chapel to beer, a fitting space for a brewery named after the patron saint of brewers, St. Arnold of Metz. The high ceiling's wood trusses are reminiscent of a bishop's miter, the tall pointy hat the saint is often depicted wearing. Light filters in through faux stained-glass windows depicting the brewing process – the stations of the cross for beer. On the way to the altar of taps are six alcoves painted by local artists who were given free rein of the three walls and ceiling, resulting in a collection of murals ripe with symbolism.

Goddesses representing malt, hops, yeast, and water dance around a fire. *Beer Garden of Eden* is a lush scene of biblical imagery. And the devil makes an appearance as a honky-tonk cowboy playing the slide guitar. One apse even looks like it belongs in an Orthodox cathedral. The artist, Nick Papas, is a liturgical iconographer whose commissions are usually for churches, not breweries. To create his piece, Papas studied the bishop-turned-hermit's life, as he wanted to represent the man behind the saintly persona. His triptych portrays St. Arnold humbly in prayer in the middle of two of his miracles: to the left, the return of his bishop ring, and to the right, the self-replenishing beer mug that sustained his faithful as they transported his remains back to Metz during a hot July in 642 A.D.

Outside, the family- and dog-friendly beer garden continues the beer-themed Easter egg hunt of hidden details in its landscaping and industrial design that blends in with the neighborhood. An upside-down brew-kettle masquerading as a silver champagne coupe creates the centerpiece water fountain. The giant hop leaves in cement and rock decorating the ground are often overlooked by lively crowds taking in the stunning skyline view.

Address 2000 Lyons Avenue, Houston, TX 77020, +1 (713) 686-9494, www.saintarnold.com, brewery@saintarnold.com | **Getting there** Bus 11 to Lyons Avenue & Maury Street | **Hours** Sun–Thu 11am–10pm, Fri & Sat 11am–11pm | **Tip** After enjoying a selection from the brewery's Bishop Barrel series, keep the art hunt going in the art car garage entrance and touring the murals covering the nearby warehouses.

99___St. Joseph Catholic Church
Hear an inspiring mariachi mass

The midday mass at St. Joseph Catholic Church in the historic Sixth Ward holds the distinction as the longest-running mariachi mass in the nation. In lieu of choir robes, members of Mariachi Norteño don black *charro* suits trimmed in shiny silver buttons, ornate embroidery, and flamboyant silk ties. Instead of the tonal sound of organ pipes, the blended harmony of the guitar, *vihuela*, *guitarrón*, trumpet, and violin resonates through the sacred space. Even if you don't know the words, the exuberant hymns will have you humming along with the fellow parishioners, who pack the pews for this Spanish-language mass.

In 1966, after Vatican II reforms to the Roman Catholic Church encouraged the use of local language, art, and music in liturgical celebrations, the bishop of Cuernavaca, Mexico commissioned Canadian priest Juan Marco Leclerc to compose "La Misa Panamericana," the standard arrangement for the mariachi mass.

After learning the music by ear during a visit to Cuernavaca in 1967, St. Joseph parish priest Patricio Flores and Mariachi Norteño are credited with introducing this popular folk music service to the United States by performing it every Sunday at Houston's second-oldest Catholic church.

Before mass begins, you can see the band members with instruments and jackets in hand, climbing the steps of the red-brick Romanesque Revival church built in 1901. Inside, as they make their way to their reserved section at the front of the church, just in front of the Virgin Mary, they shake hands and wave hello to family and friends already seated in anticipation of the boisterous mariachi music to signal the start of mass.

A second generation of musicians now plays alongside the founding members, including the two sons of Mariachi Norteño's original trumpeter, thus ensuring that the tradition will continue for another five decades.

Address 1505 Kane Street, Houston, TX 77007, +1 (713) 222-6193, www.saintjoseph.org, office@stjosephststephen.org | **Getting there** Bus 44 to Houston Avenue & Lubbock Street | **Hours** Mariachi Mass Sun 12:30pm | **Tip** In the nearby historic Dow Elementary School, Multicultural Education and Counseling through the Arts (MECA) is the largest Latino cultural center in Houston. Their annual *Día de los Muertos* month-long celebration is popular for its *ofrenda* and *retablo* exhibitions, workshops, performances, and a two-day festival (1900 Kane Street, www.meca-houston.org).

100_ Taste of Texas

Sam I am

In 1977, Nina and Edd Hendee opened Taste of Texas after declining a transfer from the now defunct Steak & Ale to a new restaurant in Kansas City. After all, Kansas City is not in Texas. Today, their steakhouse treats over 1,000 guests a day to a dining experience like none other in the Lone Star state. Locals keep returning to celebrate life's milestones because of the five-star meals and the warm hospitality, but it's Nina's passion for Texas history and her museum-quality collection of Texana memorabilia covering the walls that make the restaurant a must-see destination for visitors looking for a true taste of Texas.

While waiting for a table, you can inspect an original Texas Declaration of Independence, framed redbacks (Republic of Texas currency), Texas flag replicas, and the signatures of who's who from Texas' early days, including a rare signature of Moses Austin, the "Grandfather of Texas."

However, one of the highlights of this incredible collection is easily missed. Just to the right of the entrance is the calling card of Sam Houston, obtained from an auction where Edd was instructed to bring it home no matter what because of Houston's unique autograph in which the "S" resembles an "I." This seminal Texas figure is said to have changed his signature to look like "I am Houston," after the Allen brothers (see ch. 79 & 103) named the city in his honor, probably more of a statement on Sam than on Houston.

For a deep dive into the in-house museum, attend one of Nina's special Saturday tours, when she passionately presents her artifacts. The tours are the grown-up version of the Texas heritage presentation Nina has given to over 400,000 local fourth graders since 1985, when she first started hosting field trips almost every school day. Luckily, anyone can experience the Texas pride here – ask the hostess for an artifact guide and begin your self-guided tour.

Address 10505 Katy Freeway, Houston, TX 77024, +1 (713) 932-6901, www.tasteoftexas.com | Getting there By car, west on Interstate 10 to exit 756A TX-8 S/TX-8 N, use far left lane, make a U-turn, look for sign on the right | Hours See website for hours, tours, and event schedules | Tip From the feeder road on the way to Taste of Texas, view the lone stars and other Texas symbols that embellish the entrance ramps of the five-level stack interchange found at I-10 and Beltway 8 that tops out at 100 feet.

101_ Teo Chew Temple

Zen out in Asiatown

Dim sum, dumplings, noodles, and the latest ice cream craze from Asia can all be found in the shops and restaurants lining the streets of Houston's Asiatown. But those looking to nourish their soul head off the beaten track to this welcoming, tucked away Vietnamese Buddhist temple. The temple is part of the Teo Chew Association, which also manages a Chinese language school, a lion dance club, and special events, like the temple's Lunar New Year festival.

Glimpses of the ornate golden rooftop sandwiched between strip malls and apartment buildings guide first time visitors to the *paifang*, or archway entrance to the temple's grounds. In a fountain surrounded by the 12 animals of the Chinese zodiac, a peaceful Quan Âm, the goddess often referred to as the "Asian Virgin Mary," greets guests and believers alike as they make their way to the temple.

Wafts of incense fill the air, alerting the 14 celestial beings represented inside the temple that there are prayers and requests waiting to be heard. Whether you're trying to meet your soul mate, make a baby, or get rich, there's a god or goddess for that. Adorning the altars are offerings of fruit, joss paper (the preferred currency of spiritual beings), and bottles of Wesson and LouAna cooking oils to fuel the oil candles.

The relative quiet is only interrupted by the occasional drum beat and gong sound announcing a special offering, and petitioners rattling bamboo cups of sticks hoping to divine an answer from the heavens in response to their desires.

Unlike the somber mood of a mausoleum, the building for family memorials next door to the temple feels like a spiritual lounge. The first room is reserved for those whose dearly departed are interred elsewhere, while the second room is filled with loved ones' urns. Both rooms honor the deceased with tributes of pictures and favorite items, like packs of Marlboros and bags of Fritos.

Address 10599 Turtlewood Court, Houston, TX 77072, +1 (281) 983-0097 | Getting there
Bus 002 to Bellaire Boulevard & Turtlewood Drive | **Hours** Daily dawn–dusk | **Tip** Before
eating dangerously spicy crawfish at the popular Vietnamese and Cajun fusion restaurant
Crawfish & Noodles, pay tribute to Houston's Vietnam War Memorial located smack dab
in the middle of the restaurant's shared strip mall parking lot (11360 Bellaire Boulevard,
www.crawfishandnoodles.com).

102 Texas Art Asylum

A cure for obsessive craft disorder

Collage, quill, cross-stitch, or whittle – all crafting skills are welcome at the monthly BYOB Craft Asylum gathering at Texas Art Asylum, a haven for the craft-obsessed. Enjoy chatting with other creators and exchanging tips and feedback on works in progress – the only judgmental looks you'll get are from the resident cats. Even longer project lists are a typical result of the brainstorming sessions at this laid-back affair.

For motivation to finish a piece, enter one of the store's regular open calls for artists exhibits, with themes ranging from TV tributes to phobias. The shows are unique opportunities for budding artists to display their work – a small entry fee guarantees a spot, regardless of talent. Their calendar of events also features classes by local artists, who teach basics like needlework and more eccentric genres, like DIY memory jugs, a folk art tradition to memorialize loved ones.

Texas Art Asylum was the first creative reuse center in the state when it opened in 2010. Supplied by tax-deductible donations from businesses, institutions, and individuals, this hybrid thrift store, antique shop, and hoarder's living room is stuffed with an ever-evolving inventory, including plumbing parts, teeth, bones, decorative doodads, ephemera, shiny things, and candy wrappers, mostly sold by the pound, unless otherwise marked. You will spend hours digging through the filing cabinets filled with vintage post-cards, or traveling down memory lane looking at the old broken toys and household gadgets.

If you are looking to re-home a U-Haul-sized load of old fam-ily treasures and boxes of supplies for your unrealized craft projects eating up storage space, donations are generally accepted the first and last week of each month. The donated "Creative Resources for Artistic Purposes" will surely spark joy for the makers and artists who frequent the store.

Address 1719 Live Oak Street, Houston, TX 77003, +1 (713) 224-5220,
www.texasartasylum.com, info@texasartasylum.com | **Getting there** By car, from the
Northbound Gulf Freeway Service Road, take a right on Live Oak Street | **Hours** Tue–Sat
10am–6pm | **Tip** Find traditional hobby and art supplies at Texas Art Supply, which
claims to be the largest arts and crafts store in the country (2001 Montrose Boulevard,
www.texasart.com).

103 ___ Texas Revolution Heroes
The who's who of Texas' independence

Everything is bigger in Texas, including the schoolbooks – specifically, the hefty *Texas History* textbook seventh graders have been lugging around since the state mandated the course in 1946. While everyone remembers the Alamo (see ch. 87), there are plenty of unsung heroes of the Texas Revolution. Many of those fighters are laid to rest in Founders Memorial Cemetery, established in 1836 on land donated by Houston's founding fathers, the Allen Brothers (see ch. 79 & 100). Today, the two-acre site is maintained by the city's Parks Department. Miniature flags stand near some of the graves, while stony stumps marked "unknown" are unadorned. However, all are honored by those who come to pay respect.

The cemetery's location on Old San Felipe Road used to be considered the outskirts of the city. Now, commuters cruise down the street, renamed West Dallas, to cubicles downtown, often oblivious to the time-worn tombstones of people who enlisted upon arrival. Yankees, Southerners, and Scotsmen became veterans of the Texas Revolution. Most of the markers are engraved with heroic descriptions. Visitors will learn about John Austin Wharton, the "keenest blade on the field of San Jacinto." Commodore Henry Livingston Thompson of the Texan Navy had a funeral attended by the "largest and most respectful assemblage of citizens which has ever attended a similar occasion in this city."

Republic of Texas politicos are also represented. Seemingly destined for greatness, James Collinsworth fought at San Jacinto and served as the state's first Chief Justice. However, his campaign for Republic President as successor to Sam Houston hit rock bottom after he fell overboard in Galveston Bay following a weeklong drinking binge, ending both his career and his life. Buried nearby is Rebecca Lamar, the mother of his rival, Mirabeau Lamar, who would become the second President of the Republic of Texas.

Address 1217 West Dallas Street, Houston, TX 77019, www.houstontx.gov/parks/
founderscemetery.html | **Getting there** Bus 40 to West Dallas & Valentine Street | **Hours**
Daily dawn–dusk | **Tip** From the cemetery, you can admire the stained-glass windows in
the neighboring art deco mausoleum on the grounds of Beth Israel Cemetery, the city's first
Jewish cemetery, founded in 1844 (1207 West Dallas Street).

104 The Texas Wetlands

Call it a comeback

Saved from the brink of extinction, three native species share their amazing comeback stories as part of the Texas Wetlands habitat, illustrating the Houston Zoo's motto, "See Them. Save Them." Visitors encounter alligators, whooping cranes, and a bald eagle as they stroll along the exhibit's boardwalk complete with an ambient swamp soundtrack. The working wetlands are also home to a diverse biome of flora, insects, fish, turtles, and microscopic crustaceans that all support the ecosystem.

Two ambassador whooping cranes, Heiden and Angel, are the stars of the show with their graceful postures that would make any yogi jealous. Sadly, in the 1950s, their species was nearly decimated when hunting and habitat loss brought their numbers down to a mere 20 in the wild. But thanks to continued conservation efforts, like the zoo's partnership with the International Crane Foundation, 500 of these majestic birds now migrate from Canada to Port Aransas along the Texas coast each winter.

Not even being a national symbol keeps a bird safe from the endangered species list. Luckily for Sally, the resident bald eagle, the eagles' recovery led to its removal from the list in 2007. Guests can view this stately bird of prey up close without netting or glass enclosing her nest due to a wing injury from her days in the wild. Now flourishing once again, it's hard to believe the mighty alligator survived 150 million years before almost being hunted to extinction. The reptilian trio, Snap, Crackle, and Pop, are a cautionary tale for guests, who can see them basking in the sun beside the murky water.

Even the landscape was chosen with the zoo's conservation mission in mind. Not only do the wetland plants like lizard's tail and spider lily provide filtration and cover for aquatic life, they also attract native pollinators, another species in need of help these days.

Address 6200 Hermann Park Drive, Houston, TX 77030, +1 (713) 533-6500, www.houstonzoo.org | Getting there METRORail to Hermann Park/Rice U (Red Line) | Hours Daily 9am–6pm, last entry 5pm | Tip Visit the gators on their home turf at Brazos Bend State Park, approximately 42 miles southwest of the zoo. Just remember to keep your distance! (21901 FM 762 Road, Needville, www.tpwd.texas.gov/state-parks/brazos-bend)

105 Traders Village

Concrete Coney Island

Venture out any weekend to the city's biggest outdoor flea market, and you'll be rewarded with Houston's version of Coney Island, only on concrete instead of the beach. In lieu of a boardwalk, there's a grid of asphalt avenues creating a sideshow-meets-swap-shop vibe stretched across over 100 acres with over 1,500 vendors. This freaky flea market paired with carnival rides is far removed from the careful curation found in vintage markets and antique fairs. Here, the effortless eccentricity of the merchandise is simply a happy accident. Arts and crafts, 8-tracks and vinyl albums, anime and Renaissance attire, dreamcatchers and cowhide all commingle for the crowds of sharp-eyed scavengers and window shoppers.

Besides the treasure-hunting, there are culinary treats beyond hot dogs and hamburgers. Many food vendors sell Latin American snacks, like *elotes* (roasted corn), fruity *aguas frescas*, and the "machete," a foot-long quesadilla made popular in Mexico City. Cantinas and saloons are on-site for those in need of a beer or margarita.

Thrill seekers can climb aboard the Fleafall featuring a 128-foot drop, or the Pharaoh's Fury offering sky-high views of the grounds. Old-school amusement park types can saddle up on an Allan Herschell antique carousel from the 1950s.

The melting pot atmosphere of the flea market is best witnessed at one of the many multicultural festivals. Several events revolve around Mexican holidays and traditions: *Día de los Muertos*, *Lucha Libre* wrestling, and mariachi concerts. One of the longest running festivals is the Native American Pow Wow, where tribes from all over the US celebrate their heritage with traditional foods and teepee displays. Drums accompany dancers wearing buckskin and feathers, who come to compete for $15,000 in prize money. Hot rod car shows and Santa Claus round out the events at this something-for-everyone destination.

Address 7979 North Eldridge Road, Houston, TX 77041, +1 (281) 890-5500, www.tradersvillage.com/houston | Getting there By car, from I-10, exit North Eldridge Road, market will be on the left | Hours Sat & Sun 10am–6pm | Tip For more flea market and foodie finds, browse the stalls at Sunny Flea Market (8705 Airline Drive, www.facebook.com/Sunny-Flea-Market-165054825094).

106__ TSU Tiger Walk

Academic exercise

When school is in session, Texas Southern University's Tiger Walk is abuzz with activity. Sidewalk chalk messages advertising student clubs fade under the foot traffic of nearly 10,000 students hurrying about the 150-acre campus. Under the live oaks' shady canopy, crowds congregate for DJ sessions in front of the student center and activities sponsored by fraternities and sororities.

And occasionally, the sound of Ocean of Soul's approaching drum line signals everyone to make way for the loud and proud marching band's post-practice performance down the Tiger Walk, the university's main thoroughfare.

As the second-largest historically Black college in the country, TSU has had many trailblazing alumni and notable faculty travel along this walkway on their way to making history. Politician / activists Barbara Jordan and Mickey Leland, under the tutelage of renowned TSU debate coach, Dr. Thomas Freeman, fine-tuned their oratory skills before representing Texas' 18th District in Congress. Inside the Thornton M. Fairchild building, the campus' first structure built in 1947, you'll find the works of John Biggers, the celebrated muralist and founder of TSU's Art Department, displayed at the University Museum, along with an extensive collection of African diaspora art. Biggers' legacy also includes the walls of Hannah Hall, where art students have painted an astounding 128 mural masterpieces from 1949 to 2010.

Originally part of busy Wheeler Avenue, this half-mile section directly bisecting the campus played an active role in Houston's Civil Rights Movement. In 1960, the city's first sit-in started along the Tiger Walk, when 13 TSU students peacefully marched from campus to Weingarten's lunch counter on Almeda Avenue. Closed to speedy cars in the late 1960s after student protests highlighted safety issues, the Tiger Walk is now the ideal way to explore the heart and soul of TSU.

Address 3100 Cleburne Street, Houston, TX 77004, +1 (713) 313-7011, www.tsu.edu | Getting there Bus 04 to Cleburne & Burkett Street | Hours Unrestricted | Tip Attend a TSU home football game at BBVA Stadium to see Ocean of Soul take on the opposing team's marching band in the Battle of the Bands tradition of alternating drum line performances (2200 Texas Avenue, www.tsuoceanofsoul.com).

107 _ Turkey Leg Hut

They've got legs

Decadence is the name of the game at Turkey Leg Hut. Texas-sized smoked turkey legs stuffed and piled high with everything from dirty rice to mac'n'cheese are presented on aluminum trays sturdy enough to hold their serious weight. Your order is accompanied by boozy, brightly-colored, frozen drinks served in Crown Royal bottles, over-sized wine glasses, and sometimes watermelons. Enhancing the club-like vibe is the line that starts wrapping around the block – often hours before the doors open. Good music and pop-up tents for shade ensure that everyone is enjoying the wait.

Founders Nakia and Lynn Price didn't set out to create the next landmark restaurant in the city. While shuttling rodeo-goers from their field parking lot behind NRG Stadium, they decided to one-up the dry turkey legs from the carnival food stands with their own succulent, fall-off-the-bone version to offer to tipsy customers heading home. Neither had a culinary background, just a love for good food. The demand never stopped when the rodeo ended, so they continued to develop their concept and recipes, finally opening their Third Ward restaurant to rave reviews in December 2017. Now, alongside an expanded menu with everything from boudin balls to salads, the couple serve over 1,000 turkey legs a day – double that on the weekends.

This phenom eatery shows no signs of slowing down, as the lines only continue to grow. With famous fans like comedian Kevin Hart and rapper Snoop Dogg making sure to stop in for a turkey leg fix when in town, you never know who you'll see headed to the VIP room, including many Houston Rockets and Houston Texans play-ers who frequent the scene. But you don't have to be famous to skip the line. Make a reservation and go straight past the crowds to your table, or grab their signature Alfredo shrimp stuffed turkey leg, at the express truck across the street.

Address 4830 Almeda Road, Suite A/B, Houston, TX 77004, +1 (832) 787-0770, www.theturkeyleghut.com | **Getting there** Bus 11 to Almeda Road & Rosedale Street | **Hours** See website for hours | **Tip** Have a friend hold your place in line while you pop into Reggae Bodega to shop their selection of African apparel, jewelry, skincare products, and incense (4816 Almeda Road).

108_UH Hospitality Archives

Be our guest for the history books

Visitors to the University of Houston's Conrad N. Hilton College of Hotel and Restaurant Management can expect white-glove treatment, especially if they're staying at the student-staffed hotel. However, guests entering the Hospitality Industry Archives are the ones donning white gloves if they plan on handling a scarf worn by Elvis. Founded in 1989, the world's largest repository of "do not disturb" doorknob hangers, along with more than 15,000 items ranging from corporate documents to cookbooks, serves as an invaluable asset for industry pros, scholars, and even Hollywood.

When a *Mad Men* episode featured Don Draper harangued by hotelier Connie Hilton, the show's creators first consulted with the archive's director, Mark Young, Ph.D., to flesh out the character. As the historian host with the most, Dr. Young has helped Ron Howard and Steven Spielberg keep it real with respect to historic hotel design on movie sets. However, menus from the mid-1800s are the most frequently scanned items for culinarians curious to know what a vegetarian café in St. Louis offered as their 30-cent dinner special (savory nut loaf and peach tapioca).

Hospitality timelines are constructed though collections containing tiny soap bars, minibar contents, and company-branded credit cards, like Lady Hilton, offering solo female travelers in the 1960s women-only floors and ironing boards. In-room TV sets, reservation systems, and piña coladas – now hotel essentials – were once products of service industry innovation. You'll be hard pressed today to find a bottle of Hilton's in-house vodka brand, Darnoc (Conrad backwards), but it's in the archives.

Hilton artifacts, including personal mementos like Nicky Hilton and Elizabeth Taylor's wedding album, are plentiful. But a recent donation, the first bottle from alumni-run 8th Wonder Brewery's new distillery, also shows history in the making.

Address Massad Family Library Research Center, 4450 University Drive, Room S210, Houston, TX 77204, +1 (713) 743-5278, www.uh.edu/hilton-college/About/hospitality-industry-archives | **Getting there** METRORail to UH South/University Oaks (Purple Line) | **Hours** By appointment only | **Tip** Visit UH alumni-run establishments, Mandola's Deli, for homestyle Italian (4105 Leeland Street, www.mandolasdeli.com) and Himalaya, for Indo-Pakistani dishes created by 1989 graduate Kaiser Lashkari (6652 Southwest Freeway, www.himalayarestauranthouston.com).

109___Union Station
Going off the rails

"Build it, and they will come," must have been the mantra behind the city seal design of 1840 depicting a locomotive, though train tracks had yet to be laid in Houston. However, that can-do spirit came through in 1852, when the first two miles of railroad were laid, followed by 6,000 miles of track running through Texas in the 1880s. By 1909, construction of Houston's Union Station commenced with architectural firm Warren and Wetmore, who also were on the design team for New York City's Grand Central Terminal. Not afraid to toot the city's horn, Houston's Chamber of Commerce circulated pamphlets entitled, "Where the 17 Railroads Meet the Sea," promoting the new station as the "finest passenger station in the South."

Encompassing 13 downtown blocks, Union Station opened in 1911 with 13 tracks and a freight terminal. Business travelers, soldiers, and vacationers moved through a lobby that was adorned in marble and walnut woodwork, with chandeliers suspended from the 45-foot-high ceiling. Women had their own waiting area featuring a newfound amenity: air-conditioning. Baseball barnstorming tours arrived here too. Babe Ruth and his Yankee teammates played a two-game exhibition against the minor league Houston Buffalos in 1930.

Union Station's heyday came to the end of its line in 1974. Despite earning a place on the National Register of Historic Places in 1977, the building sat vacant for almost 20 years before making a comeback as the home turf for the Houston Astros. From a freight yard to a field of dreams, the ballpark incorporated rail motifs in its design, including a replica train that goes into motion when the Astros hit a homer. Restored to grandeur, Union Station's lobby is best experienced on a stadium tour, where you might learn the location of a Formica panel masquerading as marble in the grand hall while relishing the glamour of railroad's past.

Address 501 Crawford Street, Houston, TX 77002, +1 (713) 259-8800, www.mlb.com/astros/ballpark | Getting there METRORail to Preston (Red Line), or Convention District (Blue & Purple Line) | Hours See website for game schedules and tours | Tip The former route of the Houston Tap and Brazoria Railway is now a hike and bike rail-trail, part of a nationwide program designed to preserve unused railways. You can start the four-mile, paved pathway a few blocks from the ballpark with a connection to a longer stretch along the Brays Bayou Hike and Bike Trail (www.traillink.com/trail/columbia-tap-rail-trail).

110___USS *Houston* Bell

Relic of the Galloping Ghost of the Java Coast

Off the Indonesian coast at the bottom of the Java Sea lies the shipwreck of USS *Houston* (CA-30), a heavy cruiser that fought valiantly in the Allied Pacific naval resistance. Overwhelmed by the Japanese Imperial Navy's barrage of torpedoes, bombs, and machine gunfire during the Battle of Sunda Strait, the ship and her crew sank on March 1, 1942, just nine weeks after Pearl Harbor. The 367 crew members who managed to escape were all taken as prisoners of war, of which 299 survived to tell of their warship's courageous efforts when liberated 3,5 years later.

Taking the news of *Houston*'s sinking to heart, the citizens of her namesake city responded in a grand wartime show of solidarity, raising $85 million, enough to pay for a new USS *Houston* plus an aircraft carrier. Reports also assumed no one aboard survived the incident, so a local drive to replace each and every sailor culminated in a mass enlistment on Memorial Day, 1942. The 1,000 recruits, known as the "Houston Volunteers," were sworn in to the Navy in a fanfare celebration along Main Street with a dedication of a 60-foot ship replica, a parade, a bomber flyover, and a sendoff at Union Station (see ch. 109).

Today, the USS *Houston* Monument in Sam Houston Park honors this vessel and her men who lost their lives at sea. Atop a rosy granite pedestal engraved with the ship's history and every crew member's name sits the cruiser's original bell, recovered and restored from the underwater wreckage. For centuries, a ship's bell was rung by sailors in a distinct pattern to mark each hour to measure time at sea. Now the USS *Houston*'s bell remains quiet, but it still serves as a reminder of a moment in time. So take a seat on one of the matching granite benches encircling the memorial and contemplate the incredible story of how Houston responded to tragedy with generosity and resilience.

Address 1100 Bagby Street, Houston, TX 77002 (behind The Heritage Society) | **Getting there** Bus 40, 41 to Bagby & Dallas Street | **Hours** Unrestricted from the sidewalk, park open daily dawn–dusk | **Tip** Visit the second marker dedicated to USS *Houston* and her crew, as well as the "Houston Volunteers" and the local fundraising effort, near the location of the 1942 mass swearing-in ceremony at 1000 Main Street.

111__West Alabama Ice House

Chilling out through cool history

Spending a gloriously sunny afternoon sipping a cold one (or more), while making small talk with strangers and catching up with friends all seated around a picnic table at the West Alabama Ice House is a quintessential Houston experience. The open-air setting, reminiscent of a carport, has a few amenities, like misting fans in the summer and space heaters in the winter, but its lack of finesse is the mark of a true ice house.

Before modern refrigeration was a common household convenience, ice houses were the local purveyor of the frozen blocks needed to cool your ice box. Over time, they added other services, like groceries, gas pumps, and coolers of cold beverages. With a few outdoor tables and chairs, they also functioned as a neighborhood hangout, making it an easy transition to the local watering holes they are known as today.

It's hard to imagine that in 1928, Houston's go-to ice house was built on a dirt road in a fledgling Montrose suburb. Decades later, owner Petros Markantonis, whose father purchased the bar in 1986 when the area was rougher around the edges, has made a few modest improvements to keep up with the neighborhood's current hip hotspot designation, like local craft brew options that now outnumber domestics. But the eclectic clientele, who arrive in pickups, BMWs, Harleys, fixie bikes, and on foot pushing strollers, all still come to enjoy the ice house's chill vibe and camaraderie.

Open 365 days a year, the scene starts quietly with a few regulars but quickly resembles a festive family reunion, and then, as the hours progress, sometimes a boozy town hall. Feisty games of HORSE take place at the basketball hoop, while other patrons try to best each other at Ring on a Swing or cornhole. And if your table gets hungry, share a round of *barbacoa*, *el pastor*, and *pollo* tacos from the beloved Tierra Caliente food truck parked across the street.

Address 1919 West Alabama Street, Houston, TX 77098, +1 (713) 528-6874, www.west-alabama-ice-house.com | Getting there Bus 27 South Shepherd Drive & West Alabama Street | Hours Mon–Fri 10am–midnight, Sat 10–1am, Sun noon–midnight | Tip Sheffield's Ice House (5118 Telephone Road) serving cold beer since 1942, is one of the city's remaining old-school joints, while new ice houses, like Eight Row Flint (1039 Yale Street), revive this Texas tradition with a modern twist.

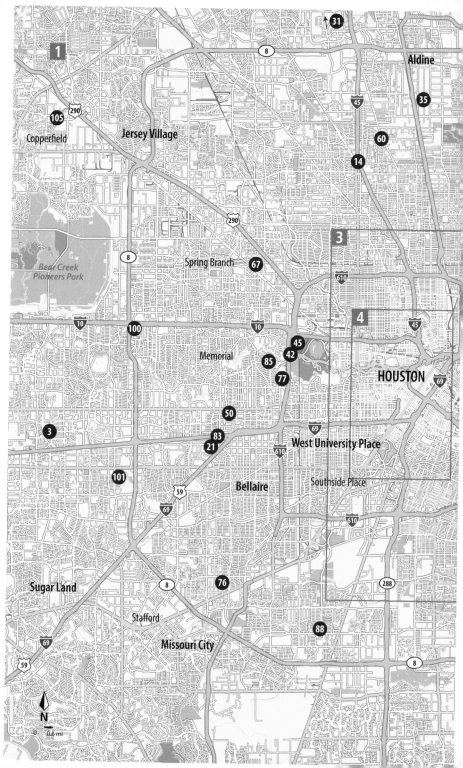

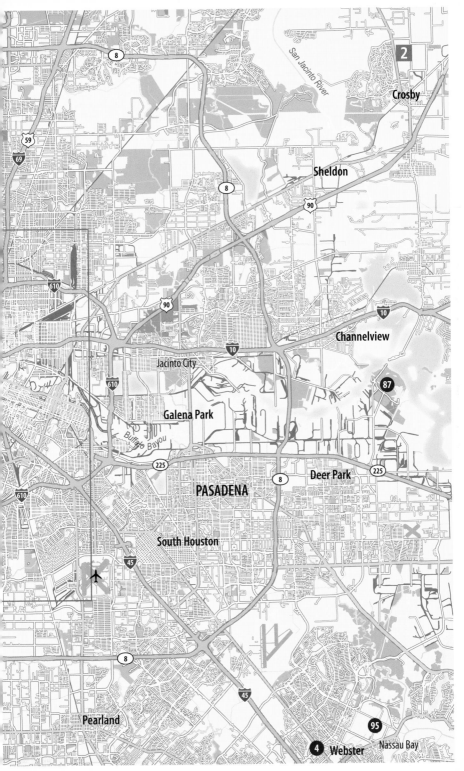

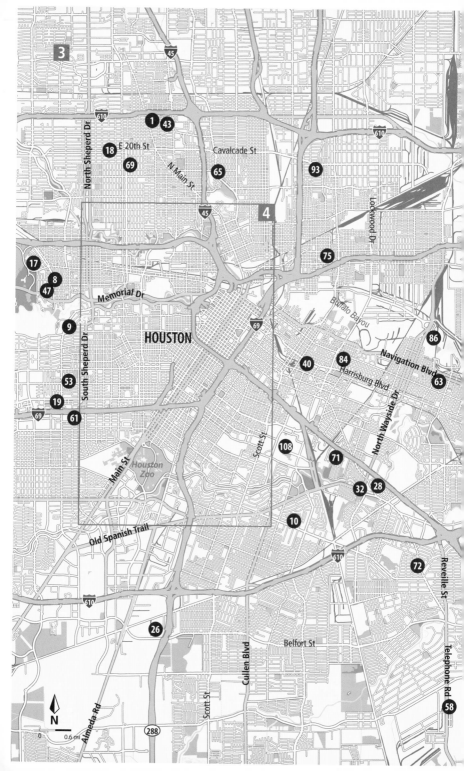

Kelsey Roslin, Nick Yeager,
Jesse Pitzler
111 Places in Austin
That You Must Not Miss
ISBN 978-3-7408-0748-1

Travis Swann Taylor
111 Places in Atlanta
That You Must Not Miss
ISBN 978-3-7408-0747-4

Katrina Nattress,
Jason Quigley
111 Places in Portland
That You Must Not Miss
ISBN 978-3-7408-0750-4

Floriana Petersen, Steve Werney
111 Places in San Francisco
That You Must Not Miss
ISBN 978-3-95451-609-4

Amy Bizzarri, Susie Inverso
111 Places in Chicago
That You Must Not Miss
ISBN 978-3-7408-0156-4

Michelle Madden,
Janet McMillan
111 Places in Milwaukee
That You Must Not Miss
ISBN 978-3-7408-0491-6

Sandra Gurvis, Mitch Geiser
111 Places in Columbus
That You Must Not Miss
ISBN 978-3-7408-0600-2

Jo-Anne Elikann
111 Places in New York
That You Must Not Miss
ISBN 978-3-95451-052-8

Laurel Moglen, Julia Posey,
Lyudmila Zotova
111 Places in Los Angeles
That You Must Not Miss
ISBN 978-3-95451-884-5

Photo Credits:

All photos © Daniel Jackson, except:

The Alley Theatre (ch. 5): Bill Saltzstein, Empty Space Images with Paul Butzi; Asia Society Texas (ch. 7): Asia Society Texas Center; Boulevard Bird Watching (ch. 11): all photos taken by Robert Flatt in Boulevard Oaks; CAMH's Open Studio (ch. 16): Jaelyn Walls; Gallery Auctions (ch. 35): photo courtesy of Gallery Auctions Inc.; HCC Central Campus (ch. 41): Joni Fincham; Houston Arboretum (ch. 42): Christina Spade; Houston Dairymaids (ch. 43): Jeff Fitlow/Rice Magazine; Houston Polo Club (ch. 45): Kaylee Wroe Photography; Ima Hogg's Gardens (ch. 47): photograph by Rick Gardner, donated in memory of Mary Gardner, courtesy of the Museum of Fine Arts, Houston; Kuhl-Linscomb (ch. 53): Dana DuTerroil; Large & Small Curios (ch. 55): photograph by Mike Rathke – Houston Museum of Natural Science; MFAH's Odyssey (ch. 64): I-Hua Lee, courtesy of Cai Studio; Post Oak Hotel Lobby (ch. 77): Fertitta Entertainment; Project Row Houses (ch. 78): photo courtesy of Project Row Houses, Houston, TX; St. Martin's Kneelers (ch. 85): photo compliments of St. Martin's Episcopal Church; Silos at Sawyer Yards (ch. 92): Jason Hall; Space Shuttle Gantry (ch. 95): courtesy of Space Center Houston; Spirit of the Bayou (ch. 97): courtesy of Buffalo Bayou Partnership; The Texas Wetlands (ch. 104): Stephanie Adams/Houston Zoo; Union Station (ch. 109): Houston Astros

Art Credits:

The Fruitmobile (ch. 6): Jackie Harris; *Books of a Feather* (ch.10): Artist DIXIE FRIEND GAY Collection of the City of Houston, Public Library *Listening Vessels* (ch. 57): Douglas Hollis © 2008; MFAH's *Odyssey* (ch. 64): Odyssey (2010), Cai Guo-Qiang, gunpowder on paper, mounted on wood as 42-panel screen 3.15 x 49.38 m overall. Commissioned by the Museum of Fine Arts, Houston for the Ting Tsung and Wei Fong Chao Arts of China Gallery; *Mount Rush Hour* (ch. 66): David Adickes, Sculptor; *I Love 3rd Ward* (ch. 78): art installation by artist Marc Newsome aka Marc Furi, Instagram: @marcfuri @ilove3rdward, I www.ilove3rdward.com; *Battle of San Jacinto* (ch. 87): Charles Shaw; *Love and Saint Arnold* (ch. 98): by the Hand of Nicholas P. Papas

First, much gratitude to our editor, Karen Seiger, who saw the passion and potential in our book proposal.

Next, a shout-out to our Houston MVPs for allowing us to pick their brains and their list of contacts: Craig Hlavaty and Jim Parsons. We are also indebted to these storytelling superheroes who generously shared their time and knowledge of uniquely Houston places from record shops to sacred spaces. Through interviews and behind-the-scenes tours, these Houstonians expanded our already wide embrace of the city through their enthusiasm and expertise: Nibu Abraham, Ameer Abuhalimeh, Mike Acosta, Marcella Arreaga, Garret Berg, Quinn Bishop, Romana Brady, Anne Breux, Peter Brown, Fern Casio, Miranda Chang, Felice Cleveland, Charles Cook, Jannette Cosley, Mark De Lange, Lawyer Douglas, Marcos Enriquez, Amy Evans, Robert Flatt, James Ford, Vinod Hopson, Father Ihnatowicz, Daniella Lewis, Jaquilyn Jack-Anderson, Don E. Jones, Genevieve Keeney, Frank Kent, Randy Lam, Debra McGaughey, Christine Mansfield, Debbie Maurer, Angie Montelongo, Shondra Muhammad, Marc Newsome, Ed Pettitt, Carlotta Ramirez, Chris Rawls, John Rittman, Tinni Robicbaux, David Ruth, Kent Michael Smith, Mark Steiner, Lisa Struthers, Austin Turner, Justin Vann, Maurice Vasquez, Robert Vasquez, Priscilla Walker, and Roger Wood. On a personal note, lots of love for our husbands and Joni's son Laurence who served as fellow explorers, location scouts, and cheering section.

Finally, thanks to our faithful desk companions, Joni's French spaniel Sophie, and Dana's English bulldog Carlyle, who request a 111 guide for dogs.

Dana & Joni

To my three best girls, Christa, Greta, and Juliet – none of this would be possible without your love and creative input. Thank you to everyone along the way who encouraged me to pick up a camera, but especially my band, my family, The Suffers. Finally, a shout out to that person I met in Philadelphia who called Houston, Texas "the most unhip part of Texas"…thank you for understanding us.

Daniel

Dana DuTerroil is a writer, lawyer, roller derby retiree, and co-owner of Trip Chandler, a two-woman team who give tours of Houston to visitors and locals. She is a Gulf Coast denizen who grew up in Houston and loves exploring her own city, one strip mall at a time. www.tripchandler.com

Houston's kolaches, icehouses, and shady live oaks convinced **Joni Fincham** to adopt the city as her hometown after living in Kansas, New Orleans, North Carolina, France, and Scotland. As co-owner of Trip Chandler, she helps visitors, new arrivals, and locals discover their own favorite pieces of Houston.

Daniel Jackson has been involved with Houston's music, art, food & beverage community for years. This self-taught photographer takes insightful portraits and has a passion for capturing the raw energy of live music. With his photos, he aims to capture the unique spirit of Houston, Texas and share his hometown with the world.